Advance Pı

"This is a powerful book, a m
make sure this book gets aroun
and this book couldn't have come at a better time. Thank you, Tim,
from the bottom of my continually growing heart."

— *PAM GROUT*, *New York Times* best-selling author
of *E-Squared and E-Cubed*

"*Life and Death* will answer many of your questions regarding those
who've crossed over. Along with many heartwarming, compelling, and
true stories from his work as a medium, Tim Braun provides answers to
the questions he is most often asked about life on the other side. Very
comforting, and helps with acceptance of death and the healing process."

— *JAMES TWYMAN*, *New York Times* best-selling author of *The Moses Code:
Emissary of Light*, and producer/writer of the film *Redwood Highway*

"This book represents an exciting look into the adventurous world of
a medium. Tim Braun's techniques for dealing with grief are superb!
As a psychic, and medium myself, I highly recommend you read this
important yet enjoyable and easy-to-read book."

— *DANNION BRINKLEY*, *New York Times* best-selling author of
Saved by the Light

"Tim Braun's new book is enlightening, healing, and a gift of understanding. I recommend it to anyone who is grieving and wanting to find
closure."

— *ARIELLE FORD*, best-selling author of *The Soulmate Secret*
and *Wabi Sabi Love*

"*Life and Death* is a very inspiring book, and specifically for those who
are battling grief over the loss of a loved one and need to find comfort."

— *CHRISTOPHER B. BUCK*, Publisher of *OM Times* magazine

"I *love* this book! It inspired me and opened my heart. Although it is
written for those that are grieving a loss, and it offers solid, excellent solutions for gaining closure, I could feel it opening up inner vistas inside
of me. I highly recommend it to anyone on a spiritual path."

— *DENISE LINN*, award-winning author of 18 books,
including the best- selling book *Sacred Space*

"*Life and Death* is full of compelling, heartfelt, honest stories and fascinating accounts of Tim Braun's personal experiences. He brings forth peace and healing for individuals, as he communicates with spirit on the other side."

— *PASCAL VOGGENHUBER*, international medium, best-selling author of
Entdecke deinen Geistführer (*The Young Spirit Messenger*)

"Tim Braun's live demonstrations are quite amazing! I highly recommend his new book for anyone seeking answers about what happens after death and where we go."

— *DAVID A. SWIFT*, director of entertainment, Pala Casino

"This book is excellent.It's an outstanding read, with some very compelling stories. It's thought provoking, as well as a transparent and balanced book. I would highly recommend this book to anyone who has suffered a loss."

— *GARY RENARD*, best-selling author of
The Disappearance of the Universe trilogy

"This book is great! It is written very clear, straight to the point. I love that. Also, Tim Braun reveals all the small things that are so important to be aware of while manifesting and healing your life."

— *SUZANNE NORTHRUP*, international medium, author of
Everything Happens for a Reason and *Second Chance:
Healing Messages from the Afterlife*

"Tim Braun is a gifted medium who offers spiritual guidance to individuals. His new book, *Life and Death,* helps empower, heal, and give closure to individuals."

— *GARY QUINN*, intuitive life coach, best-selling author,
The Yes Frequency: Living in the Spiritual Zone, and founder of
The Touchstone for Living Coaching Program®

"*In Life and Death*, Tim Braun teaches us about the true healing power of unconditional love. He provides a profound, step-by-step road map of how to ride the waves of grief."

— *SANDRA INGERMAN*, MA, award-winning author of 10 books,
including *Soul Retrieval: Mending the Fragmented Self*

"*Life and Death* offers interesting information regarding answers from the other side, teaches us to forgive ourselves, heal, and to be at peace."

— *DR. ROY MARTINA*, best-selling author of *Emotional Balance* and co-founder of Christallin Consciousness

"*Life and Death* brings comfort by sharing beautiful and deep wisdom that comes from the other side."

— *GLENN SCARPELLI*, co-founder Sedona World Wisdom Days and founder & partner of Sedona NOW TV

"Tim Braun's ability to interpret and understand messages from the deceased is quite remarkable. His journey to India and meeting with Mother Teresa was very inspirational. This book will also help individuals overcome grief, accept healing, and move forward in their lives."

— *EMMANUEL ITIER*, author of *The Invocation* book and award-winning director of the international award-winning documentary films *The Invocation* and *Femme*

"Tim has written a wonderful, and practical book on connecting to the other side. He reminds us that there is so much more to life than we can see."

— *JONETTE CROWLEY*, international author of *The Eagle and the Condor: Soul Body Fusion* and founder of the Center for Creative Consciousness

"Recently I had the fortunate opportunity to host an event with Tim Braun and watch as he worked with the audience in a profound and powerful way!"

— *REV. SANDRA DIXON*, Center for Spiritual Living, Westlake Village

"With sensitivity and compassion, Tim Braun shows us in *Life and Death* that our loved ones continue to love us from 'the other side', that the bonds of the heart are truly eternal. A healing and uplifting book."— *ROBERT SCHWARTZ*, author of *Your Soul's Gift: The Healing Power of the Life You Planned Before You Were Born*

"*Life and Death* is brimming with positive information and real life stories for those who hope to reunite with lost loved ones or simply find peace of mind. This is a book that encourages us all to look deep within and trust our own inner knowing. Insightful and inspiring, Tim Braun gently lifts the veil between worlds, offering tangible proof of life beyond life, bringing us one step closer to remembering who we truly are."

— *DR. MARY HELEN HENSLEY*, international medium
and metaphysical healer, author of *Promised*

"Tim Braun is on a journey. It is one of wanting to know, and he dared to ask. In finding his own answers, he shares with the reader through his unique gift of his mediumship, just how we can heal grief and understand the workings of the realms of Spirit. An excellent read!

— *ROBERT BROWN*, author of *We Are Eternal* and
What the Spirit's Tell Me about Life after Death

"A psychic medium selling out casinos? That's right! The time has come for spiritual work that brings comfort, hope, peace, and joy to infiltrate pop culture. Who can actually entertain crowds by healing broken hearts and opening closed minds? Tim Braun can! Tim bridges Heaven and Earth in his sold-out shows! What could be more exciting than this?"

— *AMELIA KINKADE*, best-selling author of *Straight from the Horse's Mouth:
How to Talk to Animals and Get Answers* and *The Language of Miracles*

"*Life and Death* gives stories of those seeking closure so they can move forward. This is a practical book, written with sensitivity, and is healing and uplifting. Tim, what a gift you are to the world."

— *ANNIE ASHDOWN*, author of *The Confidence Factor* and
television co-host of ITV 1's *Kyle's Academy*

"Tim Braun not only shares his stories and insight about life after death but gently walks the reader through the grieving process, offering understanding and healing. This book is a must-read for anyone grappling with life and death and wondering if love does indeed go on."

— *DONNA VISOCKY*, author of *I'll Meet You at the Base of the Mountain*
and founder of BellaSpark Productions

"*Life and Death* is an illuminating journey of medium Tim Braun. This book can help you to open your heart and heal, receive signs from your loved ones, and recognize the gifts a soul leaves when it transitions to the other side."

— *COLET ABEDI*, author of *Mad Love*, executive film and television producer

"*Life and Death* is an insightful and healing book, and I am happy to see him bring healing and closure to others."

— *ROLONDA WATTS*, actress, journalist, and talk show host

"Tim Braun's book *Life and Death* truly touched my heart. I loved to read about his personal story and his deep experiences with Mother Teresa in Calcutta. This uplifting read gives you practical tools to help you to overcome your grief, raise your frequency, and start your own communication with your loved ones on the other side. I highly recommend it!"

— *ISABELLE VON FALLOIS*, best-selling author of
The Power of Your Angels

"*Life and Death* is an illuminating journey of a medium who teaches individuals how to open their heart, tap into their own abilities, and receive signs from loved ones. Tim's message is many things -eloquent, touching and powerful. Would recommend this to anyone interested in connecting with their loved ones."

— *RICHARD AYOUB*, Emmy Award–winning television producer

"*Life and Death* offers a deeper understanding of the fundamentals of mediumship, self-healing, and connecting to loved ones. If you have lost anyone very close to you, this book is a must-read. I would highly recommend this book."

— *CRAIG CAMPOBASSO*, Emmy-nominated casting director, author,
and award-winning writer/director/producer of *Stranger at the Pentagon*

"Tim offers a wealth of wisdom in this practical handbook full of inspiring suggestions for dealing with the loss of a loved one. Amazing messages from the world of spirit make this a truly great read."

— *BRIAN EDWARD HURST*, international medium,
author of *Heaven Can Help*

"*Life and Death* is an insightful and healing book! It will help anyone with questions on grief and closure. Thank you for letting us into your life, and helping others with their unanswered questions."

— *DREW RUESCH*, manager of development,
Giant Pirates Television Entertainment

"Tim Braun's book *Life and Death* is full of heartfelt, compelling true stories from his work as a medium, and he provides answers to the questions he is most often asked about life on the other side."

— *ASHA BLAKE*, five-time Emmy Award–winning journalist

"Tim Braun's new book, *Life and Death*, is full of compelling true stories of people he has helped as a medium. This compassionate book will bring comfort and healing to many during the most important times of their lives."

— *ELLEN GOLDSMITH-VEIN*, founder and CEO, the Gotham Group

"*Life and Death* will give healing and hope to grieving individuals who discover they have not lost loved ones to death."

— *DAVID S. KIM*, founding partner and CEO of Bascom Group LLC

LIFE
AND DEATH

A Medium's Messages
to Help You Overcome Grief
and Find Closure

TIM BRAUN

To Brenda
with much Love
Blessings

 FINDHORN PRESS

Tim Braun

Published in 2015 by Findhorn Press, Scotland

ISBN 978-1-84409-678-7

Edited by Nicky Leach
Cover by Richard Crookes
Interior design by Damian Keenan
Printed and bound in the USA

Published by
Findhorn Press
117-121 High Street,
Forres IV36 1AB,
Scotland, UK

t +44 (0)1309 690582
f +44 (0)131 777 2711
e info@findhornpress.com
www.findhornpress.com

Contents

Dedication

I dedicate this book to

Christopher Moller (1975–1994)

Thank you for guiding me
and so many others
from the Other Side.

Foreword

As you will read through the pages in this book, you will come across the time when I first met Tim Braun, then a curious student of life questioning the strange occurrences which would forever shape his future. He wanted answers, and I was happy to provide him with what I knew. Now after many years I am thrilled to say that Tim has not only stayed the course, consistently listening to the Spirit world, but is finally bringing his many hours of hard work and insight from the Spirit world to the public. I could never be prouder of one of my very first students.

From the very first moment I met him, over twenty years ago, I knew he had an extraordinary, natural gift of connecting with Spirit. It has been thrilling to see Tim grow and evolve and become a bridge from this side of life to the other. He has impacted so many lives with this awareness and continues to share his insights so that many will be made aware and healed about life after death.

In this, his first book, Tim takes us on an up-close and personal journey—an adventure, really—with all its twists and turns, as he moves closer and closer toward becoming a full-fledged "messenger" for the Other Side. I love his willingness to be so candid about his life, revealing personal struggles and challenges as he comes to terms with who he really is. I have to admit: I see some of my own journey in this powerful read.

Instead of a chronology of events unfolding in his life, Tim's narrative keeps the reader on the edge of their seat as he shares his life in "scene" after "scene"—from his beginnings as a six-year-old child encountering Spirit for the first time to grappling with the overwhelming worry and confusion about his gift when he sees his schizo-phrenic brother having weekly hallucinations and breakdowns. All this wrapped around an extremely conservative Catholic upbringing.

When Tim finally decides to actively pursue his gift, life leads him to one of my demonstrations. As he is sitting in the audience, he takes us into his inner monologue of his fears and trepidations about becoming a medium while he watches me connect with Spirit in a public forum. There were even a few surprises for me, when he describes that demonstration and attending one of my workshops!

Not only does Tim share his life's journey toward becoming a medium; he shares powerful stories from some of his sitters, as they connect with their loved ones in sittings with him. These sitter stories will make you cry, and even laugh, as the sitters reveal their own struggles with healing tremendous grief and how they find ways to thrive in their new reality.

Tim shows readers how to tap into their own abilities to connect in the chapter "Raising Your Vibration." He explains how we can get messages and signs from beyond the veil from those who've gone before us. Tim's exciting narrative takes a turn when he shares his own insights about connecting with Spirit. After doing over 14,000 sittings, talking to Spirit, and delivering their messages, not only has he learned about the afterlife; he has learned about how to live life on this side as well.

I applaud Tim for writing such an honest, captivating, and deeply moving book about his life and mediumship work. I am proud and inspired to see such a gifted man have the courage to fulfill his dream and share it with the masses.

~ **James Van Praagh**

1

In Between:
Beginnings and Revelations

April 2003

Oh my God! What is that? A massive jolt shakes my body from some sort of huge explosion. I can hardly breathe. Thick smoke is filling my lungs. I see a skyscraper morphing into a giant furnace as the flames race through office cubicles, swallowing everything in their path. Now the building is imploding. My entire body is heating up.

My skin hurts. I can't breathe. "Get out! Get out!" People are screaming. I can hardly speak through my coughing. It's like my entire being is caving in on me.

Then, all of a sudden, everything turns to black. The chaos turns to silence. I can breathe again. My body relaxes. Then someone whispers in my ear. "Tell them it's Brian."

I ask the two women sitting across from me, "Who's Brian?"

The older woman starts crying.

"Should I continue?"

She nods, clearly in anguish.

I describe to her what I saw, heard, and sensed – the plane, the fire, the explosion, the crumbling building. "Does this make sense?" I ask her.

The woman struggles to speak through her tears. "Oh, my God. Brian's my son.

He was on … one of the planes … on September 11th."

The younger woman is crying, too. "Brian was my husband."

Then Brian's whispers turn into a full, rich voice: "Tell them I love them."

I repeat: "He wants you to know he loves you both. He's saying, 'Don't worry, Mom, I'm okay now.'" And then he's gone.

Brian's mother and his wife take a deep breath. Their anguish turns to peace. They smile and whisper, "Thank you." In that moment, I feel so thankful for my "gift."

Welcome to my life as a medium.

What is a Medium?

The word "medium" is defined as "in between," and that's where I do my work—in between this world and the next. For over twenty years, I've been a connector, a middleman, delivering messages from Spirit to the loved ones they've left behind.

Firemen might get burnt, cops may get shot at, but on an average day I'll be shot, burnt, strangled, and overdose on sleeping pills. Then I'll drive home from the office and walk my dogs, and repeat the same scenario the following day.

Believe me, it's not your average "gift," and being able to accept it as part of my life was a journey in itself! I didn't ask for this ability or seek it out, I was born with it. It's something I am able to do. Some people can cook, others can draw … I talk with dead people. I now find myself in a position to help others with their own journeys— and in particular, that journey from heavy grief to profound relief.

This Book

I'll begin with my personal journey of waking up to the gift, because it illuminates the valuable lessons learned by an ordinary guy coming to terms with his ability to communicate with the dead. These are lessons too valuable not to share, and they might well relate to parallel experiences in your own life.

The key lessons that have stayed with me from one day to the next are that when we wake up and trust that inner voice, we come alive. Additionally, I learned that there is indeed life after death. And I've learned that our loved ones are fine on the Other Side and that, yes, we can connect with them!

I'm going to shed some light on all of these lofty questions about the afterlife and then give you some clear, down-to-earth answers. I've accumulated a lot of knowledge over the years of listening, translating, and delivering over 14,000 messages from Spirit, and I've also learned a lot from the people who have received those messages.

If you're reading this book, it's likely that grief has swept through your life like a maelstrom. Grief has its own specific timetable, and interacting with it is a skill in itself.

Nobody grieves the same way, so in this book I've covered a range of techniques you're welcome to explore.

As part of your journey through grief, I'll guide you to connect with Spirit.

Whether or not you are considering having a sitting to connect with your loved one, these techniques of intuition, meditation, music, and creativity will not only provide relief; they will help you rise above the pain. You can even learn how to pay attention to the signs from your loved ones that are all around you.

The stories from sittings are fascinating and cover every type of loss, from friends to close family members such as parents and children. Those who've lost loved ones received precious messages during our sittings, and each of their stories is so different… so powerful, poignant, and compelling, and some are unspeakably tragic.

But above all, these stories will show how those dealing with grief found peace of mind and are even able to thrive in spite of their tremendous loss! This above all is most wonderful and gives me the greatest sense of purpose.

Purpose

The feeling of doing what we are here to do gives us a tremendous sense of peace, and every day I give thanks for finding my purpose.

According to Spirit, we all have lessons to learn. That's why we're here. Each of us has a very unique path to follow. Spirit constantly talks about the importance of raising the vibration of the planet, wanting to open our eyes to what's real and really important.

My purpose in writing this book is the same reason I am a medium: to help others heal by connecting them with loved ones who've crossed over and through sharing my stories and experiences.

Beginnings

My journey began in Whittier, California—a sunny, suburban upbringing, but one punctuated with more than enough drama for a growing boy. At this early age, Spirit revealed itself to me as lights that appeared to be dancing around people. I guess they looked more like one of those flying saucers in a horror movie, hovering over my tiny six-year-old frame.

Back then my gift seemed more like a curse, but dramatic and confusing as it was for my young mind, its presence in my life was overshadowed by an even bigger and more dramatic issue: my brother Tom was diagnosed as a paranoid schizophrenic. Tom heard voices, he hallucinated, and he had an average of three psychotic episodes a week.

A normal evening ritual of watching TV with my sister Cindy might suddenly be interrupted by Tom jumping to his feet and dragging us out the door, screaming, "We've got to get out! They're after us!" Often he had us hiding behind the garbage cans for an hour in the dark and the cold, waiting for the coast to be clear.

I'd sit there paralyzed with fear, just praying for my parents to return home.

Finally they would pull up in the driveway and do their best to calm Tom down, but I could see their concern and desperation. This grew with each successive episode, time and again. In the meanwhile, we would all walk on eggshells until Tom's next episode.

This was so confusing and frightening for a child, and at the same time I starting sensing and hearing things myself. I didn't dare tell my family for fear of being labeled crazy. My growing concern was that I was developing the same condition as my brother!

On top of that, both my parents were Eucharistic ministers in the Catholic Church. So church—every Sunday for all of us—plus a whole list of do's and don'ts. Swear words were completely forbidden, and as we grew up there were also the bonus forbidden words: gay, lesbian, condom (and of course the host of impure thoughts that went along with them).

Any discussions of a metaphysical, occult-like nature (tarot, astrology, psychic, Ouija boards) were just a big, fat no-no. In fact the mere mention of anything remotely metaphysical was forbidden.

Not surprisingly, even my little boy's brain realized, on a certain level, that I was never going to fit into this family. A child needs stability, and this "combination platter" of orthodox religion and total chaos was just too unpredictable. I felt like I was standing on top of a rolling barrel, never sure if I was going to lose my footing and have my world tumble upside down and run me over.

So I took refuge in my own little world. At the top of the hill behind our house was a fort that my other brother built for me; I'd go out there every day after school with my spoons and forks and work on it, pretending it was my very own house I was renovating.

Out at the fort one day, I heard little footsteps outside. I looked out to see this kid who looked like me: Caucasian with light brown hair. I automatically knew his name!

The name just popped into my head: Joey.

Joey wasn't there in physical form. He was like an imaginary friend, but more, in that he was an actual presence. We communicated without speaking. It was like we were talking with our minds. Joey became my best buddy.

We'd go out and play with Hot Wheels, not talking much. We didn't need to—we understood each other just fine. One Christmas, I even made a stocking for him and insisted my mom hang it with the others along the mantle, like he was a member of the family. It was the one time she humored me, and I loved her for it. She thought I was just a kid with a huge imagination.

As I grew up, it became more and more complicated to have a best friend that no one could see, and I started craving the chance to fit in. I did my best to become part of the world outside of home. But mainly I found myself content to play alongside Joey, often silently, just knowing he was there as a friend. But life is a series of turning points, and one day, everything changed.

I had finally managed to persuade some friends to come over to the house. This was big—we had G.I. Joes set up in my room. I was part of a group, tiptoeing into normality. But nothing ruins a play date faster than your schizophrenic brother bursting through the bedroom door, screaming that you're a foreign spy and yanking you out of the house by the scruff of your neck. Game over.

The next day at school was hell on earth. Kids can be cruel, and I found myself surrounded by a group relentlessly taunting me about my "weird brother." I was crushed.

It was a long walk home that night.

Then something happened that made the trauma at school seem like a walk at the park. All of a sudden I was hit by a terrifying vision: my father lying on a hospital bed, barely breathing, tubes everywhere. I had never experienced anything on this level before. It was so vivid—I even knew that the cause of his illness was diabetes.

But my mother dismissed the vision. "Oh, honey, your father is perfectly fine. You've been watching too much television."

Of course, my parents' hands were already full with my brother's schizophrenia, so they paid little attention to my growing abilities. But I *knew* what I knew—I saw visions, and this was very real to me. And indeed, my father did die of diabetes ten years later.

But as a little boy, I found myself stuck. Nobody understood me, and I was freaked out. I did not have the tools to cope or understand, so I came to a decision: I would shut out all the crazy voices and strange visions. Weird stuff, be gone! From that moment on, it was time for Operation Normal Kid.

At first, pushing the visions away was impossible; it felt like trying to stop a hurricane with my bare hands. But soon I developed an exhausting new routine: when Spirit appeared, I would look the other way. I would dodge them, shoo them away, avoid them in any way I could. I even told my imaginary friend Joey that I couldn't be his friend anymore.

And just like that, Joey was gone… along with all the voices and all the visions.

So Many Questions

My gift never really left me. As I got older it stayed with me, and while my high school friends were out playing baseball, I'd be in the library, buried under a pile of books on spirituality and metaphysics.

I also continued to associate my hidden abilities with my brother's condition. Was I going crazy? Was there something wrong with me? Was I schizophrenic like my brother Tom? So many questions and anxious worries, and no one to discuss it with!

Whittier, California in the 1970s wasn't exactly a metaphysical hotspot teeming with mediums, so my questions persisted, unanswered.

One thing I learned was that life finds a way. It turned out that Uncle Leo—my father's brother—had a great interest in the spiritual world. He sent me metaphysical books from his home in Italy, including a few on the afterlife and reincarnation that he'd written himself.

Of course, my father eventually discovered the books and had me walk them to the trash, but there was no going back for me. During my endless research into metaphysics I found Catholicism to be the opposite of what I needed. I dropped the bomb and announced to my parents I was not going to continue attending church.

Higher Learning

I was no longer welcome at my parents' home, but I embraced the next chapter of my life. I found my own apartment, got a job as a checker at Vons, a local grocery store, and transferred to the University of Southern California in Los Angeles.

Now, finally, I started to understand who I really was. I signed up for a psychology class, and during one particularly in-depth lecture on mental illness, I received confirmation that I was *not* actually schizophrenic: the symptoms were different, it would have happened to me already by this age, and so on. I gleaned enough to understand that my visions and voices were not the result of the illness I feared.

The anxiety lifted like a rising fog. Suddenly, I felt open and free to consider my gift as a blessing, not a curse!

One of Einstein's favorite quotes was, "The most important decision we make is whether we believe we live in a friendly or hostile universe." My own universe had become considerably friendlier. I had shifted my perspective, and I began to shed the parts of my life that held me back. We all have our own path, and I was now enjoying my own individual journey. Metaphorically, I had the top down and the wind in my face.

Now that I was able to regard my gift as a friend and not an enemy, my mind and spirit opened up to a new flow. You could say that my vibration was now raised to a higher level. I felt lighter and more in control.

The Dream

Dreams changed for me, too, and one in particular changed my life. Dreams are where the subconscious runs free. While our conscious mind is at rest, our inner beliefs, thoughts, and experiences process themselves. They can manifest as images and stories that make no sense whatsoever to us; they need interpreting. At other times our dreams might make more sense and present themselves as more literal. We may also receive connections and visits from other souls, receive signs, premonitions, warnings, and all kinds of traffic from other frequencies.

But some dreams just feel different. They have an otherworldly quality that stays around for days, and might be very literal indeed. One evening after a long day of classes at USC, I had one of those dreams. I lay down on my bed and fell into a deep sleep.

I saw myself in a 747 airplane, landing in Calcutta. Little fires dotted the landscape. I stepped onto the tarmac and was hit by the hot, thick air. I saw a tiny beige building: the airport terminal.

An old woman appeared, wearing a crisp white sari with blue stripes. I knew she and I were supposed to meet, and I could see a bright light around her. As I got closer, the light got brighter. I could feel its warmth.

I recognized her as Mother Teresa. She grabbed me and hugged me tight, like I was her long-lost child. I felt this incredible love and peace wash over me. Then four missionaries walked toward us and hugged me as well, like we were family. We just kept hugging in a circle. I was home, in a strange place I'd never been before. But I knew it was the home I had longed for my entire life. There were no words. There didn't have to be. We communicated with thought—powerful, loving thoughts.

I awoke to a healing presence in my room. A peaceful, healing energy – no other way to explain it. It moved toward the door and left, as if it had delivered its message.

Mother Teresa? The most famous Catholic nun on the planet? I'd just established as much distance as possible between the Catholic Church and myself, so why was I now being chosen to receive this message?

I reflected on all the messages I received from Spirit as a child, and promptly picked up the Yellow Pages. In no time, I was on the phone to the "Brothers of Mother Teresa." Seriously—the Brothers? I didn't even know there *were* brothers; I thought it was nuns only!

And here's another piece of serendipity: their building was located just *three blocks* from my dorm at USC, and they invited me to come over right away. That blew my mind, too, but when you allow yourself to be "aligned with Spirit," things begin falling into place in ways you can't even imagine.

I met with Brother Yesadas. He had a holiness, a clarity and a peacefulness, like he knew something the rest of the world didn't. I just waited for him to speak. He asked how he could help. I wasn't sure how to respond. "You had a dream to come visit Mother Teresa in India, didn't you?"

I couldn't believe it! How did he know? I tried to stay calm and simply replied, "Yes, I did." Again, this is how Spirit works. It's above and beyond our cognitive understanding.

Brother Yesedas answered a few more of my questions, and within moments I had been invited to join him in Calcutta in three months' time. I promptly took leave from my job, finished up my USC classes, got my shots, and packed my bags.

Needless to say, my parents were overjoyed I was "returning to the Catholic Church." I was too far down my own path to try and challenge their interpretation, and I simply welcomed their big goodbye party for me in the spirit with which it was intended.

Lessons from a Master

My arrival in Calcutta unfolded exactly as in my dream—the little fires, stepping onto the tarmac, the hot, thick air, and the little beige terminal building where I was met by Brother Yesadas and his group. "Everyone! This is Tim Braun!" Within minutes we were zig-zagging through the streets of this chaotic, mesmerizing city. *Beep-beep*! Cars, motorcycles, buses, bicycles, ox carts, streetcars, taxis—all swirling around each other, bobbing, weaving, and honking.

I felt no worry or concern at the strangely foreign and wonderfully chaotic environment, since I knew this was *exactly* where I was meant to be. I just allowed everything to flow over me. Flowers and fruit stands on every corner. Brightly colored buildings juxtaposed with the crowded bazaars and infamous slums. Row after row after row of tiny shacks pieced together with plastic, rags, mats, and bamboo sticks. Giant rats scurrying around. And so much human suffering everywhere, with people starving and dying in the streets.

The house was a five-story building with amazing views of the city. My small room was empty, except for a reed mat on the floor and a mosquito net, but I had everything I needed. In this minimal environment, I was already struck by how abundant I felt.

The next morning, Brother Yesadas drove me through the crazy crowded streets to the Motherhouse. This is what they called Mother Teresa's residence. We walked past the long line of tourists with cameras in hand, eagerly waiting to get a glimpse of Mother Teresa. We got to the second floor, where a group of nuns were sitting on the steps. Brother Yesadas sat me down on one of the stools next to them. He said something to one of the nuns. She looked at me, smiled, and went inside.

Three minutes later, this tiny, beautiful old woman appeared, donned in her iconic blue-and-white-striped sari and head covering. She had the brightest, biggest smile, making her seem ten feet tall. Her presence was so familiar—the same sparkling, determined eyes I saw in my dream. How do you describe meeting someone who would one day become a saint?

Mother Teresa came over and sat next to me. Her energy was intense yet peaceful. I could hardly believe this moment was real. We sat in silence. I wondered if I should wait for her to speak first. I just smiled and followed her cues, too awestruck to say anything. Then I realized words were not necessary in such a powerful moment. I could have sat there all day not speaking, just feeling the love that emanated from this awe-inspiring woman.

She started chatting about regular things! She asked how my flight was and she thanked me for coming to work at the Home of the Dying. Then she put her arm around me, and we prayed.

Action in the Name of Love

It is said that life must be experienced forward but can only be understood looking backward. I can look back on my childhood lessons and see how they guided me forward, one at a time. Each lesson provided me with another level of understanding. My lesson from this moment with Mother Teresa was that I understood love.

For the next week and a half I sat next to her every evening as she prayed for an hour. My heart was full. I knew my life would never be the same. I made a choice to listen to what that child inside me had not been able to say for many years. My own particular religious upbringing was cast into sharp relief as I learned to love fully, with an unbounded, open heart, and not to categorize others based on their beliefs and ways of life.

Out on the Streets

I started doing hospice work immediately. Each day a group of us would go out to the train station and roam the streets looking for people who were days or even hours from death. We would bring them back to the home and care for them. Mostly we focused on comforting them during their final days. I remember looking into their eyes, often seeing fear and joy at the same time.

I watched children playing together among the heaps of trash. They laughed and smiled at me, and I wondered how they could seem so happy in such poverty. I thought back to my friendship with Joey and how I had once longed for acceptance from kids my own age.

One day at the train station we found an old man huddled in a corner, barely breathing. His skin was like sun-baked parchment, draped over his bones. We gently picked him up like a fragile piece of glass and brought him back to the home to die.

Every day was like this, one life-changing experience after another, and step by step I myself began to change. While I was there to help the inhabitants of Calcutta, they in turn all helped me; I learned true compassion and true love.

Another evening a missionary ran in, yelling—a baby had been burned by oil in one of the slums. We tore through the dark streets and reached him just in time. Using just the glow from the light on my video camera, we treated his tiny, burnt body. We put salve all over him, and soon the little man stopped crying and eventually fell asleep.

I could see that once we started to help this tiny human in need, all the surrounding poverty, pain, and anguish evaporated. The only thing left was pure love.

Inclusion

I saw that Mother Teresa and her volunteers were about inclusion and acceptance of everyone. It didn't matter if you were Hindu, Muslim, Catholic, Christian, or even atheist; all that mattered was that we were all connected by our humanity. Period.

Religions around the world interpret spirituality differently based on a variance of cultural input and human observation. "Being in the moment" is known as a Buddhist attribute. "Loving your neighbor" is a Christian trait. "Following a path of righteousness" is a Muslim principle. "Devotion to God" is a Jewish staple. But Mother Teresa would simply take action in the name of love. She ticked all the religious boxes without actually trying to be religious. That was key. She would just get on with it!

I felt my years of strict religious upbringing unravel as I watched this world-famous Catholic nun teach me about real spirituality and true unconditional love. All my labels were flushed away, and I became focused solely on what was truly important.

The defining moment came when an eight-year-old boy named Jai was brought in, screaming hysterically. His leg was mangled, wrapped in an old shirt covered in blood. It had been severed at the knee by a trolley while he was playing in the street. My heart screamed out, "Why does there have to be such enormous suffering?" But Mother Teresa would not ask this. In fact, she never asked why. She focused on the what and the how.

Within just two days Jai was sitting up in bed. He squealed with excitement when

I gave him a toy car. Already he was moving past the suffering—just like Mother Teresa, he focused on the what and the how. And when it came to truly helping, I could understand that this was the focus, rather than the terrible "Why?"

A few days later I was at the children's home, walking through the corridor, when I heard a voice call, "Mister Tim!" It was Jai. They had moved him. He opened his arms, and I ran up and hugged him. I knew. I understood.

All of a sudden, I had it. The indefinable richness I felt was actually a clearer sense of purpose, which I'd attained just by being here. Soon I would return to my own country, such a contrast in terms of what "rich and successful" actually meant—fancy cars, expensive clothes, perfect cookie-cutter mansions on tree-lined streets. All these paled in comparison with this incredible, truly rich experience.

Los Angeles, California

"I'm looking for the almond milk. You only have soy milk. Where is the almond milk?"

Aisle seven in Vons supermarket couldn't be farther away from the streets of Calcutta. My perspective had changed so radically, and I was struggling to deal with the demands of first-world Los Angeles. Only hours earlier, I had been surrounded by the impoverished and needy. Though they were now thousands of miles away, I carried them in my heart like family.

India gave me a reason to get up in the morning. I knew exactly where I belonged the minute I got off the plane. Now I was surrounded by fifty kinds of bread, ten kinds of milk, rows of Hollywood gossip magazines, and I felt like a space alien had dropped me onto an air-conditioned planet of blank expressions and double-shot lattes.

"Do you have the unsweetened almond milk? I don't want the regular. I'm looking for unsweetened."

My compass spun for a few more days while I tried to adjust. But then I recalled that my dream had guided me to India for a reason.

Now I was back, and my life was finally ready to begin. It was time to shift gears; I was listening to my calling, using the unconditional love that I had found as my own "true north." I felt sure that stars were lining up and opportunities were about to appear at any moment.

And sure enough, another milestone on my journey occurred a few days later, as my gift pulled me back onto the pathway.

2

The Other Side:
A New Perspective

*"I did then what I knew how to do.
Now that I know better, I do better."*

— *MAYA ANGELOU*

Our experience is what changes our perspective; it changes what we know. You read how my childhood experiences with Spirit shaped my outlook on life, and again how my experiences in India changed my outlook on love. How about our perspective on life and death? What do we "know," based on our perspective? Is there an "Other Side"?

Our perception of life and death varies immensely across the world, based on culture, religion, and individual experience. But I've seen all preconceptions about death and heaven disappear when a grieving soul connects with a loved one. At that moment, all they feel is love.

Death leaves us with questions and brings up many feelings, which we'll deal with at length in the next chapter, "Overcoming Grief." Through my work, I can assure those who've lost a loved one that their loved one isn't actually "lost," that the end doesn't mean "the end," and hopefully I can help cast a new light on the word "death."

The Shift

In the cold light of day, our busy world of connected technology doesn't seem to have much spiritual connectivity. But increasingly a shift is taking place, with a significant global increase in spiritual connection and awareness. Increasing numbers of people are coming to know that we are indeed all connected by more than smartphones and the internet. The Other Side doesn't just begin at the "end" of life; it weaves through us from one minute to the next. Understanding this comes through experience. Our understanding of any subject will often change slowly while our life experiences unfold, changing our opinions little by little.

Sometimes understanding takes a quantum leap, and somebody who may not have even believed in a dimension beyond our material world will gain a level of understanding that changes *everything*.

With my job, I get to experience this every day with the people I meet. I watch as the curtain lifts and people realize that their loved ones carry on and are happy. It sounds unbelievable.

This rapid change in perspective can be momentarily jarring, as our brains attempt to compute something outside of their experience. Then confusion rapidly transforms into massive relief, as the person stops asking how and why and recognizes pure, unconditional love and truth.

Seeds

Someone asked me recently if I would believe in another dimension had I not experienced it myself as a child. I really have no idea. What I do know now is that Spirit is real, and our souls extend beyond this physical existence in all directions.

"But, Tim, that's fine for you to say—you talk to dead people. I can't do that, and I just don't get it."

I would never expect anyone to have an instant understanding of the Other Side, or even to believe that there is one at all, just based upon a few pages of reading. After all, it's taken me a lifetime to get to know it—and I'm still discovering new things!

So rather than trying to understand, why not just read through the experiences of those whom I've met and allow their stories to plant a seed.

Knowledge often starts this way—small, like a seed. Or like a crack in the door. We peek through and then perhaps push the door open a little wider, to reveal more of the truth.

But sometimes the door opens quickly, and knowledge rushes in. That's what happened with Jack.

Jack

"What are you looking at?" Jack asked.

"Nothing."

I tried to act normal. I didn't want to embarrass anyone, especially Robbie in front of his childhood friend, along with his wife and kids. We were in Hawaii for a few days, dining with Jack and his family in a local upscale restaurant and my visions were back in force.

This one was like reliving that vision of my dad in the hospital all over again, only this time it was an older woman over Jack's head, insisting that I give him a message. Since he was a firefighter, I thought he probably wouldn't be open to otherworldly occurrences. He saved lives, dealt in life-and-death situations; he didn't talk to people after they were gone.

I tried hard to ignore her. But she just kept talking and talking.

Now Jack was getting annoyed. "What the hell are you looking at, Tim?"

I realized I had to face this. What if I never gave him the message? How could I live with myself? 'He'll think I'm crazy—at least I know now that I'm NOT—but that's it, I'm going to tell him. Deep breath.'

"I have to tell you something, Jack. I see things that can't really be explained. And I sometimes get these messages."

Jack just stared at me.

I kept going. "The only reason I'm telling you this is because this woman's voice is getting louder and louder in my ear. She wants to connect with you. The more I ignore her, the more insistent she gets." I was thinking fast, awaiting his response. *Oh, my God. He's probably going to dial 911 or have the psych hospital come and get me.*

But Jack just looked at me and said, "Okay."

I was shocked. This big firefighter was open to the afterlife!

"It's your mother. She wants you to start the grieving process."

I could feel my heart racing as I waited to see if he was open. He just kept looking at me, listening. "She wants you to start joking around with her again."

Then I saw tears trickling down this macho firefighter's face. He turned to me, his voice almost a whisper. "How did you know?"

"Because I'm hearing her. When did she pass?"

"Just a few weeks ago. I'm the youngest of four children in a Portuguese family." Now he was sobbing. "I was the only one who used to joke around with her. At the funeral, everybody was crying except me. I held all my tears in. Today is the first time I've cried since my mom died."

Then he stopped crying and smiled. I could see he was at peace. He thanked me for his mom's message.

Grief to Relief

Jack didn't need an explanation. He didn't need to hear about Spirit, or energy levels, or have a full discussion about metaphysical theories. He simply heard that his mom wanted him to start joking around with her again and, *boom*, that was it—Jack moved from grief to relief.

This is how the window into the Other Side works. And just realizing it, feeling it, gives tremendous relief to those grieving a loss.

Usually the grieving process takes time—that's why it's called a process. And everyone deals with it in a different way. Jack would have already taken his own steps through it. But when I witnessed Jack literally jump directly into relief, it was a milestone for me. I just felt that this was what I should be doing with my life.

Learning Moment: Focus on the Endgame

Of course, at the time, I had a grand total of zero ideas on how I might fit this ability into my life. How could I help grieving people full time? Yet sometimes we don't need to know the how; it's often enough to just focus on the endgame. We just need to be sensitive enough to hear the guidance or see the signs. If it's a strong enough vision, people and opportunities are going to show up.

But you have to really be clear about what you want or you are going to miss those signs—even if they wave in your face. I was dead certain, if you'll excuse the pun, about what I wanted: "I want to use my gift to help others."

Soon I had a production job working on the Leeza Gibbons talk show at Paramount Studios in Hollywood, California, and with that came more opportunities to help others than I could ever imagine.

One person after another walked onto my path with the need for relief from their pain. And one by one, like a trail of breadcrumbs, they led me to the most incredible teacher.

Talk show host Leeza Gibbons was incredible, very empathetic, with a gift for creating and managing stimulating discussions on every topic imaginable. Of course, she was surrounded by a great team of professionals, and one of these was my co-worker Linda.

Linda

During a short break one day, I saw a faint outline behind Linda, an image of an older man. He looked at me, then looked at her and looked back at me. I knew he was desperate to tell her something and I was appointed to deliver the message. Simultaneously, I felt a splitting headache, like I'd been hit with a baseball bat.

I knew this man was desperate to deliver his message. With three minutes left on our break, I pulled Linda aside.

"First, I have to tell you I have this unusual ability to talk to people who have passed away." I looked for some sign of an open mind.

Linda looked at me. "Okay."

Then I said, "I have someone here who has a message for you. Would you be okay with me telling you?"

Linda's eyes widened. "Yes! Please tell me!"

Then I continued, "Has your father passed away?"

Linda nodded and with a shaky voice said, "Yes." The pain in my head got sharper.

"Are you okay?" Linda looked worried.

"I feel something happened with his head. Does that make sense?"

She said, "Oh my God! How did you know that? What's he saying?"

I knew she needed the message, so I just kept going. "He's standing here behind you, telling me he's concerned about you. He's saying that everything will be okay. He's telling me that he feels badly about what he did."

Linda whispered, "No one knew my father committed suicide. He shot himself in the head!" She hugged me and said, "Thank you." Then she burst into tears and ran off the set.

The assistant director yelled at everyone to get back to work—"We got a show to do!"—but I was seeing lights and visions all over the studio, above workers and guests, and hearing messages. I even heard one female voice say, "I need to talk to him." I tried to shoo her away with my thoughts but she was a pushy spirit. I quietly said, "Not now, he's working." She disappeared, thank God, but I knew she'd be back.

This is what I was dealing with. It sounds crazy, but for me it was the "new normal." In fact, if you gain understanding of Spirit and the Other Side, then it *is* quite normal.

It's just that some people have a different perspective, like being tuned to a different radio station; while everybody else is tuned to 105.1 FM, they can also hear 97.1 FM. So although I just watched and listened at first, the spirits kept after me with their messages.

Alicia

The next message was for another co-worker, Alicia. One day we were talking about an upcoming episode for the show when I suddenly saw three babies around Alicia, all yelling, "Mom!" It was like an echo of baby voices. I tried to ignore them, but they were insistent and they kept getting louder. It was so strange to have babies giving me a message. How could all of these babies be hers? None of them looked alike. One was Hispanic, one Caucasian, and one African American.

I hardly knew this woman, and I felt like I was invading her privacy. I didn't want to upset her and cause her to burst into tears on the set like Linda had. I didn't know what to do. The spiritual presence was so insistent.

Finally I said, "Alicia, I have something to tell you. Could we go somewhere and talk?"

"Sure."

So after work, we walked across the street to the park. I explained my ability to talk to people who've passed away. I took a deep breath and kept going.

"Are you okay with this?"

She said, "Yes."

I was relieved that she was open to getting a message. Then I asked, "Have you ever had children?"

"No."

"I see three babies near you. In fact, they're sitting in your lap right now. One is African American, one is Hispanic, and one is Caucasian. They're all calling you Mom. Does this make any sense?"

Alicia looked stunned. I didn't know what to think. She sat there for a moment. I could tell she was struggling with whether to tell me something.

Then she said, her voice shaking, "I know who they are. I had three abortions, and you just described my last three relationships."

I told her, "They say they understand, and they forgive you."

Alicia looked at me with tears in her eyes. "This has been hanging over me for years." I could feel the relief in her.

From that moment on, Alicia looked like a different person. She was more vibrant, more alive. This message allowed her to move on with her life, freeing her because she was no longer racked with guilt.

Drowning in Dark Energy

I started getting more and more messages for my co-workers. Soon enough it was like I became the "show within a show"—they would start crying, overwhelmed with emotion, disrupting the taping.

That wasn't the only unprofessional aspect; the guests on Leeza's shows also affected me. With one of the shows, mothers of murdered teens, I felt an overwhelming tightening in my chest just calling up one of the guests. Talking to her, I felt I was reliving the crime.

I had never had to deal with this kind of experience before, and I realized that there was a physical price to pay for helping spiritual victims; if the death had been a particularly violent one, I was going to be experiencing the entire emotional and physical trauma that took place during their transition to the Other Side.

During the show, the mother of the murdered teen began to

speak, and I got a sick, tight feeling in my body. I had difficult time breathing. I felt like I was having a panic attack. I was overwhelmed with sadness, anger, and every other emotion, as if I was the murdered son. I could see his face.

The mother of the convicted teen came on, and the feeling got worse. I wanted to run out of there, but we were in the middle of taping. As the show went on, I was drowning in dark energy, feeling like I was going through a tunnel with no way out.

Pushing the Pause Button

Sometimes in life you have to push the Pause button. I couldn't continue working on the show with these experiences flowing through me. So I quit and then thought long and hard about what was happening to me when I was receiving these messages. This was my own personal learning process about the Other Side and my place in it. Once again, my head was full of questions. I needed an expert opinion and answers that I could trust.

This pause in my vocation gave me a chance to hear the guidance and see the signs. I was able to refocus on what I wanted: "I want to use my gift to help others."

James Van Praagh and the Nuts and Bolts of Mediumship

A good friend told me about James Van Praagh. James is a renowned medium—okay, he's a legend—and when my friend offered to introduce me, I jumped at the opportunity.

We met for lunch. I was honored to be able to share a meal with someone with his amazing abilities. James was amiable, "normal," and extremely helpful. He completely identified with my situation, and he invited me to his demonstration just two nights later.

The demonstration was an incredible experience. There were

two key takeaways for me. First, it was a very clear demonstration for me of a medium connecting with the Other Side. One spirit after another appeared and related messages through James. He said, "Mediums have the ability to raise their energetic vibration, while those who've crossed over have to lower their much higher vibration to meet us halfway."

This is something I experience daily in my work. I have to slow down the vibration of the spirits as they race around! At the same time, I have to help those trying to connect to *raise* their vibration. Chapters 5 and 6 are devoted to raising your own vibration; you can do it yourself, and it will improve every part of your life!

The second takeaway of James's demonstration was that it clearly showed me how I could apply my own gift. James had a very clear process. First, he took the audience through a meditative "cleansing" in order to clean out the energy in the room.

Then he was able to connect with spirits on the spot, in the same way that I had been able to do with my co-workers on the Leeza Gibbons Show.

Just as James finished his initial meditation, I saw a young blond girl of about ten years old running through the room.

At the same time, James announced, "There's a young girl running across the room. She's about ten years old. Long blond hair. She's smiling and singing."

James called to an audience member. "The man over there in the corner. In the hot pink scarf. Yes—you. Does the name Jessica mean anything?"

"Yes."

"She is standing right behind you. She has long blond hair. She's about ten years old." Now the man was crying and nodding. He had accidentally hit and killed the little girl when she crossed the street.

"Jessica is telling me that it's okay, that she knows her passing was an accident and it's okay. She's around you all the time. She knows you were talking to her this morning, asking her to come today."

Then the man smiled, "Yes! I was. Thank you, James." Turns out Jessica had walked across the street without looking.

Then James walked over to someone else. He said, "I see a young man who crossed over suddenly. Was this your son, sir?"

"Yes."

James continued, "He's saying it's not your fault that he died. It was quick, and he didn't feel any pain." The man started to sob. "Now he's saying, 'Dad, it's okay. I'm fine.'" The man's sobbing diminished, and he started to smile.

This was exactly like my experience with Jack the firefighter in Hawaii, Linda and Alicia on the Leeza Gibbons Show, and my dad in the hospital. The transformation was so clear for those who did get messages that night. The sadness disappeared from their faces and morphed into peacefulness. There were tears, but they were also really happy to get a message from their loved one. I could see how much they needed to connect. It was a part of their healing, a really important part. They weren't just receiving closure; it was another door opening in their lives.

I knew I wanted to do what James does—to be the "middleman" who could help people connect and heal from their grief. I signed up for James's six-week workshop and became his first "student medium."

James's Workshop

Jerry, Sandy, Ken, Phyllis, Bill, Donna, and the others were all in the process of coming to terms with this gift. They had chosen to learn more about it from a master.

"I'm Tim, and I used to be a grocery checker at Von's, then I became a production assistant and guest booker on a TV talk show. I began hearing voices and having visions as a kid. I have a much older brother who is a paranoid schizophrenic. He saw and heard things at the same time while I was growing up. I was scared that I was one, too, so I decided maybe it wasn't such a good idea to talk to Spirit. I tried to ignore this ability or gift until I couldn't ignore it any longer. Now I'm here to explore it."

Next to me was Jerry.

"I sell high-end pianos. I've always been sort of intuitive. It's been getting worse lately, or better, depending on how you look at it. I was on the phone with a customer the other day and suddenly I saw his great-grandfather as a concert pianist in the Ukraine in the early 1900s. I just started blurting out what I was seeing to him. It wasn't very professional, but it turned out that he actually did have great-grandfather who was a pianist from the Ukraine. The guy was so blown away by my gift that he ended up buying our most expensive Steinway on the spot."

As James explained, this gift of talking and connecting with Spirit shows up in all kinds of people, from all walks of life, and in various ways.

And then there was Bill.

"I'm Bill Moller. This is my wife Donna. I'm a business guy. Real estate. We lost our son Chris in a car accident two years ago. He was eighteen years old. Eight months later I found that I had a gift for hands-on healing. My friends think I've gone off the rails because of my grief over losing Chris, but I know it's something much different. Donna and I both want to explore this healing further."

Just then I saw a nurse's hat floating over Donna's head, and James interrupted, "Excuse me, Donna, but I'm seeing a nurse's hat over your head. Are you a nurse?"

Donna smiled and said, "No. But that's really funny. I always wanted to be a nurse."

It was another milestone moment for me. Once again I was finding a parallel with James's process that affirmed my own abilities. Finally the Universe wore me down and persuaded me—through the umpteenth example—that perhaps I would be able to pursue a new life as a medium. In reality, it was more like the Universe smacked me across the head with a cosmic two-by-four to make me understand I was on my path! Regardless, I made a strong decision to commit to that path. I also made a choice to pursue this strong connection I felt to Bill and Donna.

The Frog's Perspective

James's mantra over the next six weeks was, "Don't try so hard! Just feel it, everyone! Learn to trust!"

Sound familiar? This brings me back to what I was suggesting at the start of this chapter: when it comes to getting your head around the Other Side, just let go, and don't work so hard on trying to understand.

It's like this. Each year my friend's children visit family in the English countryside. In the lily pond there is a large frog, and the kids follow him in a little boat as he swims around. Trying to explain the Other Side is sometimes like trying to explain to that frog that California exists—and that it has blue skies, palm trees, and surfers. The frog would say, "Don't be stupid, everyone knows there's nothing beyond the lily pond."

The frog might eventually accept the fact that there is a steel tube that flies people around the world to other lily ponds, but at a certain point he would have to suspend his disbelief and simply accept that California exists. At a certain point we have to suspend our own knowledge of the world as we know it, and take a leap of understanding that another side does indeed exist.

What the sittings and connections do is create that quantum leap of understanding. As you can see from reading the experiences of so many people, the person doesn't have to dive into the how and why of the metaphysical mechanics—they are just overjoyed to hear that their mother wants them to lighten up or their child is happy and vibrant.

James Van Praagh taught us how to listen to spirit. He taught us to tap into our senses and get out of our heads—out of our logical surface mind, where all the fear and doubt live. He helped us to become aware and trust our inner knowing. This gift needed to be honed and exercised, like our bodies in a gym. Again, we will look at this process more closely in Chapter 5: "Raising Your Vibration," because it applies to everyone, not just those who are full-on mediums.

Meet the "Clairs"

Connecting with Spirit through "the clairs," or "the clair senses," addresses the intuitive abilities that correspond with the senses of seeing, hearing, and feeling. With James, I focused on clairvoyance (clear seeing), clairaudience (clear hearing), and clairsentience (clear feeling). It turned out I was able to connect using all three. My gift was getting stronger and stronger.

Mediumship is definitely a craft. A medium needs as much evidence of Spirit as possible before ever giving a message. If Spirit isn't made real for the loved ones, they won't recognize Spirit is actually communicating to them.

Personally, I was so used to these random messages coming at me that I didn't know there was an actual process to this. It was a relief to have more of an instruction manual. So much of this work is about trust. And to let the trust come through, the way has to be cleared.

The next level deeper is learning to turn off the "spirit spigot." Seriously, the stream of spiritual messages coming my way used to be like one of those uncontrolled fire hoses in a cartoon, spraying water all over the place until somebody grabs it and brings it under control. Turning off the spirit spigot involves focusing energies so that the medium isn't constantly bombarded by so many different voices and visions.

Learning Moment:
The Sum Total

Finishing James's class, I looked back on everything that had led me to this point. It's important in life to understand that we are the sum total of all our experiences—even the perceived "bad ones" can find a way to benefit us.

For example, enduring the death of loved ones as a child may mean that one is better equipped as an adult to help others through similar experiences. Equally, hearing confusing voices as a child, in a heavily Catholic family and with a schizophrenic brother, can also work out as a positive!

Finding out I wasn't actually schizophrenic, experiencing the prophetic dream, spending time with Mother Teresa in India, my fledgling medium skills developing at the Leeza Gibbons Show, and even being a Von's supermarket checker—everything had conspired to make it all happen perfectly.

The experiences of my life had led me to this point of discovering my pathway. I interned with James for a year, studied with more mediums in the UK, and then discovered that my next-level teacher had been sitting right next to me at James's workshop.

Bill Moller, Superhero

As I noted above, Bill was a fellow student at James's workshop, and he found his path in quite a different way. His son Chris was killed in tragic car accident just blocks from their home. Chris was eighteen years old.

The grieving process is a unique and personal experience, as we will discover in the next chapter. Bill's grieving process was certainly unique. He felt Chris's presence more each day, and knew he was being prompted by him. Soon Bill felt he was being guided to create a place where people with gifts like his could explore their abilities of connecting with Spirit in order to heal others.

In 1996, Bill opened the Spiritual Healing Center in Torrance, California. Bill worked with two other healers, Teri Williams and Carol Ross, and together they formed the center as a nonprofit; Bill refused to charge anyone for a session.

The center is a wonderful legacy to Chris and remains a testament to Bill's remarkable abilities. I was privileged to be given the freedom, trust, and space to practice my skills in this professional setting and develop into the medium I am today.

Every day at the center, I would sit in the corner and observe Bill placing his healing hands on the physically sick, who would come in with various diseases, conditions like cancer and arthritis. He literally has a healing touch—it's one of those unexplained metaphysical skills that can appear so "sparkly" and mysterious, but it's really a form of science, and the results are very real. As I watched, I started to sense messages more clearly than I ever had before.

For the first few weeks I held back a bit and just watched Bill doing his thing. He saw auras and would often ask me, "What do you see, Tim?" But I didn't see anything. I really tried to see the auras—squinting my eyes tight, then opening them wide hoping to see what Bill saw. But I got nothing.

Then one day while he was healing a woman, I just blurted out, "I see your son."

Both the woman and Bill looked at me, startled. All the fear and doubt inside me disappeared, and I just kept going. "He died at thirteen years of age."

It was indeed the woman's son. She started crying because she was so happy (and surprised) to have made a connection with him.

Bill asked me, "How did you do that? How did you know he was thirteen?"

I shrugged my shoulders and said, "Because he told me." I dished it right back to him: "Can't you see it, Bill? Can't you hear the voice? He's right there talking!"

Bill stared at me. He knew exactly what I was doing, and said, "No, I don't see anything, Tim."

We both looked at each other and smiled. We just got each other. Bill's ability to sense illness, heal people, and help others to transition to the Other Side complemented my ability to get messages from those who'd crossed over.

We made a partnership and even completed 15 cable shows together in the 1990s called *Looking Beyond*, where I was the host of the show.

Learning Moment: Push Through

Working with Bill became the home and family I'd been searching for my entire life. But this was a decision to join together based on my intuition. It's important to listen to that inner voice throughout our lives. Sometimes it whispers gently, and other times it smacks us with a cosmic two-by-four, but it is always right.

Usually Bill put his hands on the person to see where the problem was, and I would see Spirit behind them. Bill would look over at me and ask, "So, Tim. You got anything to add?"

Then I would jump in and say something like, "I'm seeing a female directly behind you. She passed away a year ago suddenly. Does this make sense to you?" And the person would say, "Yes! That's my wife!"

Then Bill would add in his two cents about the auras he saw. It was like choreography! Knowing all the details from the Other Side in each case helped Bill pinpoint what needed to be done with each healing. The person would leave feeling better physically and emotionally. But I only felt confident enough to do this work if Bill was in the room.

Then one day Bill pulled back from helping me. A woman named Peggy had come in for a healing. I was in my usual role—sitting next to Bill as his metaphysical sidekick. Bill looked at her and then looked at me for a moment, very determined, and said, "Don't you see it, Tim? The colors around her?" Again, I saw nothing.

Then Peggy said, "Tim, I hear you're a medium. What do you see?"

I wasn't used to being put on the spot. Minutes passed as we all sat in silence.

Nothing. I even looked over at Bill for help, but he left me high and dry. Good old Peggy was still sitting there, the essence of patience. She looked up at me, waiting for something to happen. *Nada.*

Then Bill piped up, "That's it, and I'm tired of you stealing my energy. Go in the other room with Peggy and work on her yourself!"

Stealing my energy? I looked at Bill and assured him that I was never stealing anyone's energy—or words to that effect—as I confidently led Peggy next door.

Thankfully, Peggy was still the patron saint of patience as she sat across from me. We looked at each other and smiled awkwardly. Inside, I was clutching at straws. This was one of those classic freakout moments that happen before someone has a breakthrough.

It doesn't matter if you're a writer, a chef, a lawyer, or a landscape gardener—we all go through a series of "blocks" when training to get better at something, and this was a nice big one for me. I was terrified of messing up.

But here's the thing: there is always a path forward. My personal light bulb moment was simply a flash of insight to *trust* and *to have faith*. It doesn't matter what your background is or what spiritual direction you may lean toward, trust and faith are two of the best tools you have for life's tricky moments.

So the way trust and faith manifested themselves was to at least start a meditation.

I took action—faith is nothing without action.

"That's it, Peggy. Good. Just breathe in and out. Clear your mind." A woman appeared over Peggy's left shoulder.

"It's your mother, and she's telling you to be happy. That she's okay now." Her mother went on with more information only Peggy would know. Peggy began to nod.

"It's her! It's my mother!"

Tears began streaming down her face. As it turns out, Peggy had been hoping for her mother to come to her that day (I had never met her before, so I had no idea), and she came through strong and clear.

After the sitting, Peggy said the experience changed her life. It opened her up. She learned to surrender and trust. She learned that there is an eternal peace and that life continues. Most importantly, she learned that there is hope.

Peggy told some of her family members and friends about me, and it was official: I was now a full-time, full-fledged medium. Bill was thrilled. Then he said something that really hit home. "You just didn't know that you knew, Tim."

Learning to Fly

I realized that my time at the center was not just about me having a place to practice the early stages of becoming a medium; it was about my own healing, which had to take place in order for me to strengthen myself. I needed to heal from the pain of feeling like an outsider for so much of my life. Once I found a home and people who accepted me, I felt whole.

That's what we're all looking for—a sense of belonging. In a wider circle, knowing there is this Other Side gives us a sense of belonging. The reality of healing is manifested through unconditional love. Mother Teresa taught me that one: the most powerful healing comes when we give unconditional love to others.

At the moment I felt my independence as a medium, I remembered a wonderful poem by Christopher Logue, titled "*Come To The Edge*":

> *Come to the edge.*
> *We might fall.*
> *Come to the edge.*
> *It's too high!*
> *COME TO THE EDGE!*
> *And they came.*
> *And he pushed,*
> *And they flew.*

Sometimes we need a push. Bill Moller pushed me and I learned how to fly.

Perspective

The lessons I learned about my own abilities in connecting to the Other Side are forever with me, to be built on and referenced as I help others move through their grief and find closure.

The more we learn about the Other Side and its appearance in this life, the more our perspective changes. Like the frog in the pond, we are limited by the confines of this life until we glimpse something beyond our familiar world.

You've seen the quote, "We are not human beings having a spiritual experience; we are spiritual beings having a human experience."

Well, this isn't just a bumper sticker for me—it's my life. It's a perspective that guides my everyday existence.

One person who knew all about perspective was Charlie Chaplin. Chaplin was convinced that storytelling was "all about where you put the camera." He said, "Life is a tragedy when seen in close-up, but a comedy in long shot."

Chaplin's point was that if you see a man fall down in the street, it's very dramatic if you are close to him. In this close-up view, you feel his pain. You see the expression on his face when he falls, the impact as his cheek smacks on the sidewalk, the immediate pain, the loss of pride, the smudge of blood, the torn clothing. It's not fun. We share his hurt.

But how about your friend across the street who watches the same man fall over? Oh, the humanity… A shoe flies in the air, his world turns upside down, passersby stop. It looks like he's okay. We don't see the details but, well, it was kind of funny, especially now that he's brushing himself off and we know he's all right. Our reaction changes based on our perspective.

Similarly, when we move our viewpoint and see life from a different perspective, we may find that what we labeled a tragedy could be interpreted as something different.

What if your loved one committed suicide, or was killed in a violent murder? The residual feeling is that if that soul then exists in some kind of afterlife, then it must remain a very unhappy, tragic soul, in the same way that the loved one who is left behind is unhappy.

But you should see the relief when somebody hears that their lost loved one is actually telling them not to worry from the Other Side—that they are joyful and forgiving and loving! The shift in perspective and the feeling of relief is immediate—and massive. "You mean they're okay?"

Yes, they're okay. We can know they're okay. Life can start again. Things can move on. But what about the person who has not had the opportunity for a sitting? How do they deal with their grief?

3

Overcoming Grief

Grief is a sledgehammer. It's the wrecking ball that knocks you sideways and then sits on your chest. Grief is the "super-heavy." You can't get out of bed. You can't stop crying. It will interrupt that nice lunch you were having with a friend. It will show up at your business meeting unannounced, as a rolling wave of pain and hurt. Grief is an untrained dog that will jump on your bed at 2 a.m. and race through your mind until dawn.

Without some kind of additional understanding, we find ourselves open to attacks from grief. Grief is often seen as something to be fought, to be resisted, to be endured, and to be "gotten through," like some kind of minefield or bramble of thorns. Too often, we just hang on and keep our fingers crossed that we will emerge intact, with our sanity in place.

The next two chapters, "Understanding Grief" and "Managing Grief," go into the grieving process in depth, and offer some rungs up the ladder to bring you out of the darkness.

You can't manage what you don't understand, so we'll start with that. By knowing, by understanding, by looking grief in the eye, it loses its power to damage you and hold you down.

We think we understand grief because most of us have experienced it in one form or another. But what do we really understand? I want to take you into the nuts and bolts of grief, because some of the most persistent obstacles to moving through it are sitting in plain sight. Then, once a basic understanding is in place, you can start to process grief, using a number of different methods that we'll discuss below.

One Note:
Professional Help

A self-help book is no substitute for professional help. This book is meant to provide understanding and a way forward. As mentioned before, this book plants healthy seeds one at a time, but a garden takes time to grow. Your need for help might become immediate if you become increasingly depressed or hopeless, consider not being here anymore, or rely heavily on substances. The journey through grief is often a tough road, and there's nothing shameful about seeking professional help.

Planting a Seed:
What If?

In the last chapter, I discussed changing perspective in order to understand the Other Side. With this chapter, I'm suggesting a different perspective in order to understand grief. What if you embraced grief? It might sound nuts, but seriously—try letting grief in through your door, accepting it into your life as part of the experience. Know that it will be there.

When you understand grief and look at it, then you can process it. Grief needs to be understood and then it needs to be expressed. It needs to be given time to unfold, not held back like water behind a dam. Just know that you will feel lost, and that sometimes you'll be in a huge amount of pain; if you loved deeply, you will grieve deeply.

Extra understanding can help put grief in its place. If we change our perspective, grief is something we can learn to understand, accept, and even embrace with love. Love dissolves all barriers, all sense of separation. It releases grief's powerful grip.

It's the same approach as Mother Teresa; she used unconditional love in every aspect of her life. I could not do what I do without unconditional love. For me, working without unconditional love would be like trying to watch TV without electricity. It's the life, the energy, the be all and end all of our universe.

The Nuts and Bolts of Grief

What are the characteristics of grief? The following is a list—far from exhaustive, as I'm not a fan of laborious explanations. What I *am* a fan of is getting help to people who need it, as soon as possible.

If you're standing in the self-help section of a bookstore a couple of weeks after losing someone dear, you're not going to feel like thumbing through a bunch of wordy manuscripts, trying to find something that could help. You're looking for something quick and clear. If you're emotionally wounded, you need an ambulance, not a thesaurus. Plus it might be hard to read anything right now, so I've kept it short, just a few pages, and as clear as possible so you can flip back through this section in a tough moment.

You can do more research on each section, but the following headings will get you going:

What to Expect

During the early days of grief, there are several physical reactions. Expect tiredness, nausea, difficulty sleeping, fear, panic, and stomach pain. You'll feel disbelief, shock, anxiety, and confusion, and you are sometimes likely to feel that you are going crazy. Crying is woven with anxiety, and both are fuelled by emotion.

Crying

The crying comes easily, out of nowhere. It's an overflow of different emotions that have woven together and filled us up to the point at which our bodies make a physical release and we cry.

Anxiety

The anxiety stems from uncertainty, questions that race through our heads: What will I do now? What could I have done to prevent this? What am I feeling? And so on.

The Emotions

Grief is a Pandora's box of unchecked emotions. It's not just the searing weight of grief itself that pulls us down; grief also brings a whole bunch of uninvited guests to the party: shame, anger, fear… All these unwanted buddies will gatecrash your life as soon as grief barges in through the front door.

Pining and yearning for your missing loved one is a huge one. The need to see them, hold them, hug them is overwhelming; when this meets the thought and realization that they are never coming back, the result is a howling pain. Crying, deep sobbing, and exhaustion. You're shattered.

Motivation

You have no motivation. It's hard to concentrate on anything, to absorb information, or make decisions.

Tolerance

Emotions are hard to control, and you'll be less tolerant of others. There's a feeling of being powerless. This makes us feel out of control. And when we feel out of control, it makes us feel vulnerable. This in turn can create the urge to throw a huge tantrum as a reaction.

Guilt

There are a bunch of things you could feel guilty about after a death. It might be that you didn't get a chance to say goodbye. Perhaps you don't think you spent enough time in a hospital or with that person in general. You were "always busy." You might be beating yourself up for letting your teenager drive on the night they died in an accident. Guilt is good buddies with fear, and is one of the uninvited guests who gatecrash once grief has arrived. Again, to deal with guilt, write out specifics as to what you feel the most guilty about.

Regret

Regret goes hand in hand with guilt—things that were said, things that went unsaid, things not done, and unfulfilled plans.

Anger

Anger is closely related to guilt and regret. Anger is a common reaction to loss. My friend's mother found herself frequently angry after the death of her husband of forty years. With anger comes blame, and she was blaming everyone, from the company that supplied his easy chair to the mailman to well-intentioned friends who interrupted her day. She threw herself into a letter-writing process, responding to every sympathizer who wrote to her, and became angry with that, too.

It was only when the fog cleared and she gained some distance from the actual loss that she was able to look back and understand: anger had been one of the emotions that emerged with her grief. Anger creates the illusion of being in control. But you're not in control, and that's okay. Let grief do its thing; let it happen.

Shock Deaths

Sudden deaths are different. This is because they challenge our assumptions about life at a very basic level. The death of a loved one is never easy, but at least a long illness or a death from old age will give us a chance to adjust to the event when it finally happens. But death from suicide, homicide, infant death—these create a shock that is in sharper contrast to our preconceptions about how life would or should unfold. And the greater the gap between what happened and how we thought life would turn out, the harder it is to come to terms with the death of a loved one.

How Long Will I Feel Like This?

The first six weeks after a death, the grieving loved one will often report feeling as if they were on autopilot. They will also report feeling even worse after about six weeks, just when they felt they should be starting to adjust. The reason for this is that the body releases adrenaline and various chemicals during the initial period of shock to help you cope. After about six weeks, these chemicals recede back to normal levels, and so you start feeling worse.

This also happens to coincide with the period in time when you find yourself a little less busy and distracted by the funeral, responding to letters, and when attentive friends and relatives begin to recede back to their own lives. Nice timing. Even more reason to have a structured approach to coping with grief.

Wave Pattern of Grief

There's a recognizable pattern to grief: it comes in unexpected waves. Different things can trigger these waves—a smell, a favorite song, a significant date—and you never know when one of these will set you off. Expect the unexpected. Understanding this gives you more control and keeps you from thinking you're going crazy.

Write down particularly intense triggers, as well as the easier ones where grief came anyway. The ups and downs become less intense as time goes on, but keeping track of what causes these waves of grief can help you predict what kind of pattern lies ahead.

What *Not* to Expect

"I thought that the more time went by, the better I would feel." In our modern world, we have come to expect things to follow a predictable and immediate pattern. Grief has none of that. If you think you should have stopped crying by now and be better within weeks, then the process will be harder to deal with. Change your expectations. If you have a better idea of what to expect, you can manage your feelings better. Because it comes and goes in these waves, the only thing we can predict about grief is that it's unpredictable.

Be Patient

If you have been waiting for a chance to develop your patience, now is a good time, because grief cannot be hurried or rushed; it knows no sense of time. Anyone who's spent time in the garden knows that nature takes its own course, and that is always the best course. There isn't a gardening book in the world that will tell you to grab that tulip and pull it hard—"Oh come on, grow!" Nature won't be rushed, and the grieving process is as organic as any other. Take it easy. One day at a time. Be prepared for grief to take its own course, and like that tulip, allow it to take its own course.

This requires time, so give yourself the time to grieve. That time can be spent in various ways: letting the anguish out, letting the tears flow, or writing out feelings, memories, thoughts. You can set aside time to take walks, learn to meditate, and read. (See below for more actions.)

Grief is not an illness with a prescribed cure. You don't "take one of these and call me in the morning" with grief. We're a quick-fix culture, led by technology and fuelled by impatience. We swallow a pill, we click "return," we are used to instant gratification, and we're generally impatient to get things over with and move onto the next chapter. Not so with grief. Grief don't roll like that. Grief will be done when grief is good and ready.

The best thing you can do is understand grief and get in sync with it; then you will know its ways, as unpredictable as they may be, and it will take its natural course through you, rather than leaving a destructive path across your life. Grief isn't over in an instant. And it's not a black-and-white, here-today-gone-tomorrow issue. Grief is more like a range of colors and tones that vary day by day. Don't expect a leap from heavy to heaven in one fell swoop. Just let relief come to you one step at a time. Before long, you'll look over your shoulder and see how far you've come.

Another very important step is:

Give Yourself Permission to Be Sad

This one sounds completely obvious—I mean, hello, doesn't the sad come with the grief? That's like the wet coming with the water. Well, in fact, this is one of the biggest obstacles that people put up for themselves.

Here in the West, we are more likely to equate sadness with weakness rather than see it as a normal human response. We often fight the urge to be sad, but it is so important that you allow yourself to feel your pain—that is how you properly grieve the death of your loved one. And I'm sure that is what they would tell you from the Other Side.

Some cultures make a point of very demonstrative, open displays of sadness during a grieving process. This is actually healthy. Crying is good for you. Don't fight it. Let go of that urge to control. Crying is actually the body's way of releasing stress-induced chemicals. So allow yourself to feel sad and cry. You'll live longer.

4

Managing Grief

You can overcome grief's hold and that feeling of powerlessness. First, you need to express the grief, then you can shift the balance of power by taking action.

Express Your Grief

There are many ways to express your grief. We just talked about crying. But what about simply keeping a journal? Writing is not just an excellent way to release thoughts and feelings; it can almost be a form of meditation.

"Oh, write, you say, Tim? I can't even get out of bed. How can I lift a pen and open a book? And write what, exactly?"

Writing in a state of grief may take some getting used to. Left to your own devices, you're likely to open a blank page, stare at it, and not be able to write a word. You may want to write but you can't. You want to go for a walk, but you can't do that either… you can't even eat. It's the same with anything. Grief creates inertia, and quite honestly you'd rather just curl up in a ball, thank you very much.

Timed Writing

So get yourself a buddy: the stopwatch. Seriously. A great technique to just get writing is to do what's called a "timed write." Pull out your pad, set the timer for fifteen or twenty minutes, and just write, nonstop. Don't stop moving that pen, even if you are just doing squiggles and loops while you wait for the next thought.

Just do it. Write a list of what you feel, what you remember, what you never want to forget. Write a story. Just let it out. Writing out your experiences and feelings is like a purging process. It gets what is inside your mind out onto paper. Commit to it; it *will* make a difference.

Make Time

For those of you with busy careers or children to raise, it's not always easy to carve out time for grief. But don't do it for just a couple of days and then fall back into a hectic lifestyle, because your grief will get stuffed away in the corner, unprocessed.

I urge you, with love and compassion, to make time to grieve, and make it a regular part of your day. Grief is better out than in, and creating the time to do the above will help you move forward.

Grieving the Monsters

By the way, these processes don't just apply to those of you who have had wonderful relationships. Your relationship with the person who died might have been full of pain and unresolved issues.

I know people whose childhoods were made a misery by one particular adult. When these adults died, these people might have expressed relief that the monsters were no longer living, but at the same time the deaths brought up a different kind of grief. The methods above can also help process these feelings.

The point is, if you keep your pain and grief inside, it can build toward psychological and physical problems down the road. Taking action is the best way to move forward.

"Thanks but No Thanks"

We all know people who offer unsolicited advice—some of them may even be our friends. Watching a friend grieve makes some people uncomfortable and prompts them to offer "helpful advice."

You might hear: "You've got to get on with your life." They may advise you to "pull yourself together," "stop crying," "think of the children," and so on. God bless them. They mean well, but just be aware of them, send them a silent blessing, and return to your own personal expression of what you are going through. You can take the initiative and tell them what you need. Take a little time to reflect and consider what those needs are, or perhaps talk your needs through with a particularly compassionate friend.

Write this stuff down. It really helps clear the fog of grief, and helps you create a clear path for yourself through this period. Then you will have clear boundaries for yourself and can graciously refuse a friend's suggestion that you need to get out of bed, go dancing, or buy a motorbike.

Take Action

Action is the key for handling grief. Read that again. Action is the *key* for handling grief. It's so important I wrote it twice. No one else can grieve for you. You are the one who has to move through it. It hurts, I know—there's no app for it, and we can't outsource it offshore or hire someone to grieve for us. The best way to move through grief is to take action.

At first it will be hard; you will be dragging yourself into motion. Remember the "timed write"? Find a way to get into motion, whether it's going with a friend or imposing a time limit. Like a rocket taking off from the launch pad, overcoming inertia will be tough at first but will become easier as you get going.

And in the same way that expressing grief will be different for each person, taking action, whether it's by talking, painting, or exercising, will be different for everyone, too. Try a few different things to see how what works.

Start with small steps, just an hour a day. Creating a schedule will help. Sometimes you need to do nothing. But more often than not, engaging in some kind of activity will help the process, whereas staying at home alone will make it worse. If a friend invites you to go out and do something, just say yes. Make a list of the activities you used to do each day, before your loved one died. Ask yourself which one of these would be easiest to resume. Incorporate your daily to-do list into these activities.

Eating

One of the first things that goes when we experience grief is the eating process. Not only do we lose our appetite, but the emotional attachments to mealtimes, places at the table, and so on are often too much to bear. You have to put fuel in your car, otherwise it sputters to a halt. Similarly, you have to put fuel in your own tank. Feed the machine. Sometimes you will have to force yourself.

To make a difficult process easier, choose meals that are easy to make. You might make more than you need and freeze the rest. Invite someone over, limit your alcohol intake, and eat many fruits and vegetables. This is basic stuff, but in an emotional crisis you need tips and a road map.

Exercising

Again, start with a little a day and build it into your routine. Do something you enjoy. Take a walk—alone or with a pet or a close friend. If you want to move onto something more strenuous, such as team sports, just be aware that you may not be up to the commitment or social interaction yet.

Sleeping

Another basic need that is affected is the ability to get a full night's sleep. Meditation and yoga are excellent natural helpers to put your mind at rest. Exercising in the morning or evening can help. A warm bath or listening to soothing music can guide you to a more relaxed frame of mind.

One common complaint during periods of grief is waking up early and then not being able to get back to sleep. If this happens, you can read a favorite book, try warm milk, or listen to gentle music or a guided meditation.

Also consider a "mental guide" for yourself to allow you to take these recurring worries and put them out of your mind for now. Write down a brief description of what's bothering you and promise yourself you will attend to it in the morning. This way your brain places the worry into a different compartment, enabling you to focus on the most important thing right now: getting rest.

But above all, don't *panic* about not sleeping. Again, it's just one of the attributes of grief you have to accept for now, knowing that it will pass in time.

The Road Map

Grief is a combination platter of loss and change. The nuts and bolts of change are different from the spiritual care you will be attending to, but they do need to be addressed.

These changes may involve everything from moving, financial decisions, or changing employment. Paying the mortgage, upkeep of the house, selling the car, finalizing the will, changing bank details, and so on are all things you might have to face after the loss of a loved one.

This stuff is no fun on a normal day, and during grief it can feel like a cruel burden, salt in the wound. Make it easier on yourself by creating lists, writing it all out, and getting someone to help.

Create your road map for dealing with these changes and find someone reliable and capable who can coach you through them. List the issues that you need a solution for. Then make a list of possible solutions, with positives and negatives for each. Finally, go through the consequences of each solution and ask yourself whether you can live with them or not. If not, go back and think of a different solution.

You'll feel a sense of accomplishment when you create the foundations for the new chapter of your life. This will allow your body and mind to deal with the emotional side of grief, knowing the decision-making process is being taken care of.

Self-Care

Looking after yourself is essential during the grieving process; otherwise, grieving will take its toll on your mind and body. Counteract the possibility of negative effects by taking positive actions. In turn, these constructive, positive actions will help raise your vibration. This is key to creating your own connection to Spirit, and is so important I have devoted the next chapter entirely to it.

Where to begin? Try pen and paper. Create a list of things that you consider helpful during your journey through grief. Some suggestions, in no particular order:

MUSIC: The universal language. Music that you adore, or that your loved one adored. Listen on headphones, in the car, or around the house. Have your favorites. Immerse yourself. More about this in Chapter 5.

YOGA: Even if you have never done yoga, a few introductory classes will be of enormous benefit. At the very least, they will get you out of the house and introduce you to a peaceful and healthy form of exercise and spiritual release. You may find yoga a very real form of physical release for stored energy and grief, as it literally opens up your energy points. Find a gentle yoga class or one that works for you.

MASSAGE: You'll have a lot of built-up tension, and massage is a great way to keep yourself healthy while releasing stress and toxins.

MEDITATION: I will introduce a basic approach to meditation in the next chapter. There are so many different methods, and you can take guidance from a resource you discover or try a few different approaches to find the one you feel works best for you.

EXERCISE: Get out and do something that appeals to you, even if it's just a fifteen-minute walk.

CREATE A BOOK: Create a book in memory of your loved one. It's not as hard as it sounds, and joyfully assembling your favorite memories, pictures, and notes can be a very positive part of the journey, bringing out that unconditional love that you then find yourself passing on to others.

FIND THE RIGHT BEREAVEMENT COUNSELOR: Okay, nobody is perfect, but meditating and listening to your inner self can guide you to that one professional who "just feels right."

FIND THE RIGHT BEREAVEMENT GROUP: Listening to like-minded people with similar experiences can be very uplifting. It is a giant release to just unload your story on a group of strangers. Online bereavement groups can be even more helpful; for some people, anonymity can help the process move along more easily.

BE WITH FAMILY AND FRIENDS: Talk to the right friend who is willing to spend time with you and listen. Sometimes our most accessible resource is a close friend, as close as a telephone call.

BE ALONE: This is imperative for some people. Long walks, or even taking a personal trip far away, is another option for self-care. Take a holiday! Seriously, if you were ever going to just get away somewhere, now would be the time. Just take off somewhere and clear your head—walk, cry, write, read, and swim.

BE ASSERTIVE: Setting boundaries for yourself and learning to say no to suggestions or requests that either don't feel right, or that you're just not up to right now, will help keep you from feeling overwhelmed. Saying no is a complete sentence and doesn't make you a grumpy old so-and-so. If you are used to putting others' needs before your own, try putting some of your own needs first—it's part of the new you.

GET A PET: A fluffy dog or cat you can hang out with can do wonders!

VOLUNTEER: Giving resources or time to others will lift you up and take the focus off yourself. While helping others in need, you will receive the thank-you gift of new perspective on where you are.

Taking care of yourself will become easier as time goes on and you move through grief. And as you do, you can begin to feel your spirits rise. Hope emerges, however faint. This leads you to the next stage of spiritual and emotional healing: raising your vibration.

Twelve More Steps Toward Moving Beyond Your Grief

1. Surrender

We can't control the fact that we've lost someone we love. And we can't bring them back. But we can move forward into a more peaceful state of being. Surrendering is letting go of the pain (even for a moment) so you can live in the present. It knows that something bigger than ourselves is protecting us. Whenever you feel that wave of grief, surrender to it. When you're overwhelmed, see the word "surrender" in your mind's eye. Say, "I surrender" to yourself. It will act as a reminder to let go for a moment.

2. Forgive Yourself

You may have guilt around your loved one's death. You may feel responsible, blaming yourself for not doing enough. You must remember that this was their life's path. To move through the grief it is important to forgive yourself so you can free yourself to heal.

3. Connect with Your Loved One

If you are open to the idea that their spirit is alive, there are many ways to connect with your loved one. Going to a spiritual medium is a great way to do that. Many bereaved people have found solace in the messages they receive from their loved one on the Other Side. You can also connect with them on your own, in your daily life.

The key is to send them love and light energy. As you heal yourself through the grieving process you may find a deeper connection to your loved one. There may be signs and messages that occur. Stay open and aware. Talk to your loved one. They want to connect with you if your heart is open.

4. Nurture Yourself

It's so important to take the time to take care of yourself. Remember you are still here and there is life ahead of you—there is joy to be experienced. Do the things that make you happiest right now. Even if it's something small like going for a walk, watching a favorite movie over and over, and even making your favorite dish and eating it with a loved one.

5. Meditate

There is nothing more powerful we can do than meditate. It quiets the mind, energizes the soul, and creates a more peaceful state of being. It can be the anchor that gets you through your day. Find a meditation that works for you. From Passage Meditation to Transcendental Meditation. Try to practice it every day, even if it's for a few minutes. Start with five or ten minutes, and work up to longer or more frequent sessions.

6. Dream of Them

When you go to sleep, ask your loved one to visit you in your dreams. Think about them. Send them love. It is thought that when we dream of our loved ones who have passed on, it is their way of communicating with us.

7. Create

Keep a journal, paint a picture, take a photograph, create jewelry, sculpt, sing, act, even create a memory book of your loved one. Whatever your creative passion or interest is, tap into it. even if it's a very small creative project. Creating connects us to our deeper selves. That's where the healing is.

8. Garden

Gardening is giving life. The process of watering and nurturing is healing. Watching a plant or a garden grow will create a peaceful state of mind. You can even grow your loved one's favorite plant or flower. Talk to your loved one while you are gardening. Feel their presence.

9. Exercise

When we exercise, it releases endorphins, which expedites feelings of happiness. Find an exercise you love to do. The deep breathing associated with exercise can also release pent-up sadness and trigger tears that need to come out. Emoting is a healthy sign and can help get you through the grieving process.

10. Ritualize

Creating ritual around the memory of a loved one is a powerful way to keep them with us. After all, that's what most of us want. We miss them. We want to feel their presence. The ritual can be whatever you want it to be. It can be an altar-like corner in your home. Or you can create an "active altar" by doing an activity as you remember them. Perhaps something they loved to do. Or you both loved to do together.

11. Pray

Asking for guidance and support is important now. Prayer is a powerful way to attain that. Remember when you pray, don't just say words in a rote fashion—feel your feelings; that is where the power is. Just the practice of saying a prayer can help you navigate your grief, because it is an action step and a tool toward healing.

12. Seek Support

Getting outside help from bereavement groups and therapists is important and can help you deal with the stages of grief. It's especially important if you find yourself in an ongoing depression. This is a fragile time and it's essential that you seek the help you need.

REMEMBER. This is *your* journey. This is a time to explore who *you* are. The grief you are experiencing does ease with time. Take all the time you need to get through this life challenge. Be gentle with yourself. Surround yourself with positive, loving people and great experiences, and you may find that your heart has opened to a wonderful new life as you carry the memory of your loved one forever.

5

Raising Your Vibration

We've looked at the nuts and bolts of grief and how to deal with it. Once you have started taking solid action to deal with grief, the next thing you can focus on is raising your vibration. This process is ongoing, and can take place either before or after a sitting.

I know what you're thinking. *Vibration? Hmm, sounds like some hippy thing, Tim. I see sandals, brown paper, and crystals. What's vibrating exactly? Are we all shaking inside? Come on. I'm grieving. I need answers.*

What Is Vibration?

I didn't even know what the word vibration meant until I started learning the details of mediumship. Vibration is a level at which we are able to give and receive energy. Have you ever met those people who seem to be calm and in tune? They seem to be able to ride through life's waves with more ease. They are usually going through life at a higher vibration, which means they have a stronger spiritual connection. They repeatedly practice becoming more in touch with the Other Side—that which surrounds us and runs through us in this life.

Many of the techniques for raising one's vibration are the ones I practiced with James Van Praagh and Bill Moller during my medium apprenticeship: meditating, breathing, clearing our minds. Like the exercises to move through grief in Chapter 3, immersing oneself in these to achieve real effect requires a certain amount of commitment. You need faith that your actions will bear results. But when you feel those results within and observe your life change on various levels, these exercises will get easier and become lifelong habits.

Clearing the Path

My own personal experiences in raising my vibration involved clearing my path, unburdening from my past, and focusing on self-forgiveness. Immersing yourself in these processes will further ease the burden of grief. It also prepares you for connecting with the loved one who has moved on. You may be considering preparing for a sitting. I usually recommend waiting three months after the death of a loved one before having a sitting to connect with them. Even if you are not currently thinking about having a sitting, raising your vibration clears your connection to the Other Side.

People come to see me because they want to connect with their loved ones. They are missing that person terribly, they are pining for them, and they would love to have just one more moment with them. They want to know if their loved one is okay on the Other Side.

After getting messages from their loved one during a sitting, the sitter will often ask me before they leave, "Can I connect with them on my own?" The answer is "Yes!"

Remember, your loved ones want to connect with *you* as much as you want to connect with them. And you can do several things to make that possible.

It all starts with developing your intuition—something that we're all born with. And when we're open to it, we can increase the chances of receiving those precious signs and messages.

Intuition

"I was *just* thinking about you." "I *knew* that was going to happen." These are the pointers to our intuition. Intuition is the flash of insight that guides us like an internal GPS. Even the toughest business leader will admit to having a "gut feeling" about something. One successful record executive even named his company Gut Reaction.

73

It's an ability we all have, whether we acknowledge it or not. But our busy lives distract us. Find and refine your intuition. Turn off the cell phone, create a space of time without electronic media, and meditate. Find a way that works for you. Start with just focusing on your breathing. Empty your mind. This may take some practice, but make time. The more you do it, the easier it is.

Pay Attention

Keep a notebook. Live in the moment. How do we do this? Again, meditation helps, and we'll get into that below. For now, just start by being aware of how "in the moment" you really are. We are so used to checking email, tapping our phones, texting, talking, calling, overstimulation, and overthinking. On top of that, grief gives us the worries and concerns that we didn't even consider before our loved one left us.

We think of that person who is no longer with us. We miss them terribly. Then we worry about how we will pay the bills. We worry about how worried we are and how worried we will become. Fear feeds on fear, and a cycle of anxiety and even panic can ensue. It is said that if we are living in the past, we are depressed. If we are living in the future, we are anxious. If we remain in the present moment, we can be at peace.

A pro tennis player mentioned a trick he uses to stay in the moment. When he walks out to play an important game, he touches a spot on the ground just outside the court. That is where he leaves all his worries, everything about the outside world, and for the next two hours those worries stay there while he focuses on his game. When the game is over he makes a point to touch that same spot and "pick up" his old worries again.

Write things down. Get them out of your head and on paper. Make a list of worries, with the biggest concerns at the top. Purge your mind of these distractions and make a point of staying present.

Find things that work for you. Get creative. Think freely and allow yourself to discover a trick that works for you.

Learn how to control your mind, or your mind will control you. Most of our experiences in life and how we react to them are under our own control.

Love Will Bring Us Together

Love is the great connector. You can focus on someone who lives on the other side of the world and send them love, and on some level they will feel it. This is not some fuzzy concept—it is actual science. A carefully controlled scientific demonstration conducted in Washington, DC in 1993 involved approximately 3,000 people meditating for peace for two months. By the end of the study, figures revealed a 23.3 percent drop in violent crime. The odds of this happening by chance were less than two in one billion.

Peace is a force. Love is a force. They work like science. Yoga is also science. Our western world is just opening up to the concept. And what do you need when you are dealing with science? Logic, born out of common sense. Similarly, mediumship is spiritual science. There's an action and a result.

So let love be your action. Send love, not negative, "crying out" thoughts. Remove those roadblocks.

Actions

Find a picture of your loved one, or a special item. Put it next to you or hold it while thinking loving thoughts about them. Do things that bring you joy. Spend time in a location you love. Take a walk with an animal they loved. Place yourself in the most beautiful part of your environment. Find somewhere that they loved and spend time there. It might be a favorite corner of your garden, a park they loved, or a special walk you did together.

Spend time with others you love. Surround yourself with the love and friendship that brings out the best in you. Love is our connection to the spiritual level, the Other Side. It is void of fear, of preconceptions, and busy thoughts of "what if."

The more we pursue this path and conduct our own "spiritual research," the clearer it becomes that on the spiritual level nobody is doing anything wrong or making any mistakes. Trying to accept this feels like that frog in the lily pond. *What? No. How?*

This will be especially hard to contemplate if your loved one was taken suddenly, or by violent means, or was a child. "Why did they have to go *then*?" It seems so unjust, and at first look the idea that "everything happens for a reason" is blown out of the water.

Drawing ourselves farther into love creates understanding on a deeper level. Our perspective shifts, little by little. Don't try to answer all your questions in one go. Know that love is the answer. Dive into it.

Self-Forgiveness

This is a huge part of clearing the path, so I'm going to devote a healthy chunk of text to it. When we have found fault with an acquaintance and wish to make amends, we have to forgive them. If we don't forgive them, it's impossible to proceed with any kind of meaningful relationship; there's always something unresolved in the back of our minds, and that colors any thought or discussion we try to have with them. It's like driving with the parking brake on.

Likewise, we can't enjoy a fulfilling relationship with ourselves if we don't do the same thing. We need to forgive ourselves. We have to make amends with our own minds.

The warped perspective we have on our personal history, our guilty brains, and our toxic shame—they all conspire to limit who we are and what we can become. Left untreated, our "unforgiving selves" will hold us down. Healthy and active self-examination requires action.

Start by looking in the mirror every morning and tell the face looking back, "I love you." This is tremendously hard for some of us … and what does that tell you? The negative beliefs you hold about yourself will hold you back. They will also be projected outward. This in turn will affect the way you connect with others, which will affect the way your life unfolds.

These negative beliefs fly against the truth of your authentic self, yet somehow they have been integrated into who you believe you are. That's why it is so hard to love yourself. You might be carrying childhood resentments, or doubts about your trustworthiness or abilities, all stemming from childhood punishment. You probably don't even understand or remember the sources of this negative energy. But the results manifest themselves as we move into adulthood and reinforce them over time.

What about someone who has passed on? How do we manifest forgiveness if the person isn't here in the physical? You've lost a loved one. There is so much you wanted to say. So many things you wanted to clear up. Maybe you didn't tell the person how much they meant to you and that you really loved them. Perhaps they hurt you deeply and you're still carrying it with you.

Remember, forgiveness is more about you than about the person you need to forgive. Even if the person whom you need to forgive is still here, it's not always necessary or possible to confront them. This is about you confronting you. So it doesn't matter if the person has passed on. It is critical that you forgive yourself if you wish to heal the grief of your loss and let it go. In that process, you are letting yourself go.

But what about forgiving yourself because you think you caused their death? First, remember that each of us is on our own path. We're in our own movie, and we make choices. We cannot control someone's destiny. The first step toward forgiving yourself about a loved one who has passed on is to surrender and accept their destiny.

Forgiveness is forgiveness. Even if the individual is alive or passed on to the other side. Remember, it's about *your* path and *your* experience. You can choose to forgive and be free to live in the present, or stay stuck in the memories of what you've done or what someone else has done to you in the past.

Seven Tips Toward Manifesting Forgiveness

1. Be Clear About What Happened

Understand why you feel hurt and be clear about the circumstances that caused the hurt. You can share it and get clarity with a friend or a therapist.

2. Change Your Attitude About Forgiveness

Remember that forgiving is about your own healing. It is an opportunity to be your best self. Focus on the benefits of forgiveness, not on the drudgery of having to forgive.

3. Take Baby Forgiveness Steps

This is important! Even the tiniest egregious behavior needs forgiving. The more we get into the forgiving habit, the more we build our forgiveness muscle and can cope when the bigger issues arise. Start right now! Think of someone who may have done something like not returned text messages or cancelled plans at the last minute for no good reason. Start forgiving them. The sooner you start forgiving the freer you'll feel.

4. Use Prayers, Mantras and Affirmations

Prayers, mantras, and affirmations are all great tools in manifesting forgiveness. The key is to find the right practice for you. They serve as your anchor, protector, and healer. Make them a daily habit.

5. Write a Letter to Yourself

Write a letter to yourself about the hurt, the situation, and the person who hurt you. Let your thoughts and emotions flow. This is just for you, so it doesn't have to be perfect. Just write continuously. Writing is a powerful way to get to the deeper part of us.

6. Keep a Journal

In addition to writing a letter to yourself, a daily journal is a great way to move from not forgiving to forgiveness. It can be a powerful motivator to keep forgiving.

7. Visualize Forgiveness

Visualizing a situation in your mind first can have a powerful effect on the subconscious. The following visualization will help you feel the feeling of forgiving, which in turn will help you manifest forgiveness.

Sit in a quiet room, or you can put on some meditation music. Imagine a dark, heavy door in front of you, slightly ajar. Feel the anger, resentment, and hurt you have toward that person whom you need to forgive, it may even be yourself. Now imagine those feelings going through that door. Close the door. Feel its heaviness as you hear it shut.

Now imagine yourself turning around. Before you is a giant picture window with beams of glorious light shining through. See the window opening. As it opens, feel the powerful, freeing feelings of forgiveness rush toward you and right through you. Feel the tremendous healing as the liquid light permeates every part of your being as you forgive this person. Bask in this new positive energy. Feel the joy because you have manifested forgiveness.

Can we all forgive? Absolutely. Don't we all want someone to forgive us if we have caused them hurt? Then we all have the ability to forgive another who has caused us hurt as well. Start making forgiveness a habit—an integral part of your life. Let go of the past so you can start living in the present. Tell a new story. And look forward to the next opportunity to forgive. And you'll find that you will be forgiven as well. When we realize that we want to spend the rest of our lives full of joy, fulfillment, and freedom, we will want to start forgiving as soon as possible

Guilt and Shame

Two things very strongly linked to self-forgiveness are guilt and shame. I mentioned them in Chapter 3, because they also happen to be two of the close friends that grief brings to the party.

Guilt is a feeling of remorse over something we did or should have done. "I should have spent more time with Dad." "I shouldn't have let Robbie drive that night." Shame is remorse about the kind of person we are. In short, guilt is the feeling that we *made* a mistake; shame is the feeling that we *are* a mistake.

Guilt is an internal compass that guides us to do what is right, so don't feel too bad about having some guilt! If we make good judgments, we build self-worth and integrity. Write a list of ten things you feel guilty about doing, and list how much of your guilt is appropriate or not appropriate. You might be surprised how much your guilt is reduced just by completing this exercise.

Shame is something that really affects our self-worth. Self-loathing is surprisingly common, and it is so frustratingly effective in limiting who we can become. We need to see ourselves as the individual masterpieces that we are, so it's worth taking the time to identify and demolish as much shame as you can.

I'm going to spend a little more time on shame, because toxic shame not only can block your path, it can kill you. The mind-body connection is powerful, and many terminal illnesses are the result of a lifelong build-up of core negative beliefs.

Try the following:

1. **Discover your negative beliefs by writing them out**.
   "I'll never be…" "I'm always going to…" "I can't ever seem to…"

2. **Identify their source**.
   As far as you can, remember whose voice convinced you that each of these was true. Just know that most parents are themselves wounded beings and almost subconsciously pass on negative traits and feelings that the child isn't enough.

3. **Weigh these beliefs**.
   Write them out and make a comparison—which are false and which might be true? Most of the beliefs may be false, but some of them could be true. So what? No one is perfect. Embrace these beliefs for what they are, and do *not* judge yourself.

4. **Get rid of these beliefs**.
   Stop giving them your energy. Turn them around. Zap them by making the negative a positive. Were you accused of being unfocused or scattered? Consider the strengths of being creative and able to think outside the box. Were you labeled antisocial? Reflect on how you prefer your own company and choose that company carefully. The Other Side always has another side. Recast these "beliefs" in a positive light.

5. **Transform these beliefs**.

What if you have some seriously negative attributes, like the accusation that you are mean or cruel? Could you accept these parts of yourself and see them from a spiritual perspective? This kind of radical self-acceptance comes from seeing a wider view. Write out all of your attributes, positive and negative, and make it a lighthearted and joyful statement of who you are, warts and all, take it or leave it! By viewing your existence as part of the greater whole, you see that you fit into this world perfectly. You are part of the fabric of the universe.

If this section resonates with you, then please take some time to expand your research. New approaches to self-forgiveness are emerging all the time. It's a wide topic, and we've just scratched the surface here.

Feeling the Feelings

Finally, simply understand that you are the sum total of all your experiences, whether these are viewed as positive of negative. I spoke about this before, but it's worth repeating here because it's so important.

There is such a tendency to label everything as a "good" or "bad" experience, and to try and "airbrush" various life experiences into oblivion that might be perceived as "not positive." A situation we might consider "bad" in the western world could be something that a person in a distant culture is praying for! And experiences build us, strengthen us, and give us new skills for life.

You don't have to be many decades through life in order to understand this. An example is a friend of mine who happens to be a very talented hairdresser. When she was just a teenager, the school psychologist wanted to prescribe drugs to "help" her through her parents' divorce. At the ripe old age of fourteen, this girl had the presence of mind to tell her counselors, "Hey, maybe I am *supposed* to be feeling these feelings right now!" She refused the medication. Today she is a successful, confident woman with a breadth of life experiences under her belt.

Of course, medication is sometimes necessary, and I'm not refuting that. But sometimes the emotional experience that we consider "pain" is actually capable of building us up—if we embrace it. It can make us stronger and provide us with skills that we can use to help others.

Change your outlook on your experiences and what you consider "bad." This will reveal new levels of joy and self-acceptance, and give you a big, bright chance to forgive yourself. This will also give you invaluable tools to deal with self-forgiveness, self-worth, guilt, and shame.

To that end, I'm going to throw out another seed, one that extends that idea of embracing a "bad" experience.

Planting a Seed:
Embrace Grief

Here's a thought: anything we don't love runs us and limits our inspired actions with fear.

Entertain the idea of loving the things you don't like, including the grief, including the pain, including those bad memories.

It might sound crazy. But when you consider that what you don't love runs you, ask yourself, do you want to be run by grief and all the things that it brings: fear, pain, and sleeplessness… ?

Put your focus into meditating, clear your path, and then, yes, embrace the grief. You will find grief will loosen its grip on you. It's the same principle as "Love your enemies"—we've been hearing that one for 2,000 years, and yet how many people do you know who practice it? Exactly. It's uncommon. Don't take another 2,000 years to dip your toe in the water on this one. The reason more people don't try it is because it's counterintuitive and just plain scary. It's one of those leaps—a change in perspective that requires some letting go.

Acknowledge and make peace with your fears, or they may secretly rule over you. When you learn to love the blocks and messages of sickness that appear to be in your path, you will conquer your own fears and move forward in your life.

Again, I'm just planting a seed. This book is full of them, especially the ones that deal with changing your perspective. Go back through the book later, discover more of these seeds, and just let them sink in.

6

Through the Darkness
and into the Light

In this chapter, you will find solid skills to take you higher out of grief and also sustain you at that higher level for the rest of your life. The side effect of these skills is that you will also become more able to connect with Spirit.

Grief brings pain and fear, which we label as limitations. But your limitations are rooted in one place, and that is inside your head. From this bed of love will grow self-worth; self worth is a wonderful counter to the sagging energy of grief.

Grief is a process of rebuilding. Building yourself back up is a form of spiritual creation. Maximum growth occurs at the border between order and chaos. The grieving process will feel like total chaos at times, and you'll wonder about your sanity. But remember to see this as a part of the natural reaction to losing your loved one.

This might not be the first time you have experienced crushing grief. But let this be the time that allows you to walk through the darkness and into the light. Once you learn that your heart and soul guide you to whatever you need to resolve a situation, you'll know that there really are no problems; only opportunities to learn another lesson in love.

Meditate to Communicate

Meditation is the single most powerful and simple step toward developing your "sixth sense." Meditation quiets the mind, helps us focus, heightens our awareness, and puts us in a calm state of being. It creates a fertile environment for connecting to the Other Side. By tapping into our subconscious, we find ourselves on the pathway to our soul, where our best self and our intuition reside.

If you take nothing else from this book, cut out the next two pages and stick them on your refrigerator, because meditation is powerful beyond description.

Strength isn't always loud. Strength can come to you by sitting silently and tapping the most powerful force in the universe. Words don't do justice to the potential strength of this silent method of connection. In fact, words are clunky substitutes for this higher level of spiritual communication. Children at the preverbal stage operate largely through pure intuition and internal energy, partly because they are still fresh from the Other Side. When kids begin the process of language and the cognitive brain takes over, their powerful intuition moves to the back seat.

One day, perhaps intuition will be sustained through childhood. The Dalai Lama said, "If every eight-year-old in the world is taught meditation, we will eliminate violence from the world within one generation." In the meantime, it's never too late to rediscover this joyful level of connection.

We hear countless people from all walks of life speak of how meditation completely changed their lives; at their own starting point, these people all found one particular type of meditation that felt comfortable for them.

You can meditate by simply focusing on your breathing, using prayer, clearing your mind, visualizing, or just sitting quietly. Another way to meditate is through "passage meditation" (where you focus on the words of a meaningful passage of writing).

Which type of meditation should I choose, Tim? Will I end up like Gandhi? Do I need a yoga mat and a loincloth? Stop. Forget the clichés. Meditation is accessible and practiced around the world by everyone from children to CEOs. The one thing these people have in common is that they started with just one breath and now make meditation a daily habit.

Listen to music industry super-producer Rick Rubin: "The more time you spend being quiet and looking in, your intuition grows and you trust it more," he said. "Messages come if you're looking for them. Through meditation, I developed the skill to know what to ask for. It's like a 'knowing.'"

Remember the "knowing" I spoke about at the beginning of Chapter 2? As we learn, ascend, and increase our vibration, our knowing continues to change. The abstract knowing that Rubin refers to is well documented in academic research on meditation.

"Meditation creates a state of equilibrium, of peace, of calm, of openness, that really allows an opportunity to be both an open canvas but also a calm and neutral canvas," says Vered Hankin, research assistant professor at Northwestern University's Feinberg School of Medicine. Hankins conducts clinical research on meditation.

"Meditation is a jumping off point for knowing," she says. By quieting the chatter in the mind, "every once in a while you have a moment of connection, a moment of insight, a moment of the real feeling like it comes from some other part of you that you might not be accessing if you weren't in that connected space."

Simple Meditations

Volumes of books have been written about the many different types of meditation; they fill libraries around the world. Meditation is a huge subject and I could write a whole book about it alone. But for now, I'll create an introduction for you that can get your foot in the door.

Here are some simple meditations. Ideally, sit in a comfortable chair with both feet flat on the floor. The duration is usually from a few minutes to twenty minutes or even an hour. I like to do twenty minutes a day.

Breathe

Simply breathe in deeply, three times.

Clear Your Mind

Focus on your breathing and allow any thoughts to pass through your mind. Give them an internal smile and send them on their way. Do this repeatedly for at least ten minutes.

Visualize

Imagine a giant white light (or a golden ball of energy) hovering over you. See it slowly descend through the top of your head and make its way through your body. Imagine bathing in the healing light as you relax every part of your body. Remember to breathe in and out.

Passage Meditation

Spiritual teacher Eknath Easwaran developed this meditation saying, "It transforms the thought process and uncovers our deepest capacities—all within the context of an active modern life."

Memorize a simple spiritual passage or text, such as "The Prayer of St. Francis," "The Best" by Lao Tzu, or a favorite poem. Say each word to yourself slowly, focusing on the word, not its meaning.

Mantras

The purpose of repeating a mantra is to ease anxiety, quiet and steady the mind, and to connect us with our inner self. Gandhi called a mantra "the staff of life." They are like an extension of meditation (and can be used in meditation); yet different, because you can say your mantra to yourself while walking down the street, or wherever you are and whenever you need to. Say it as often as you can. A mantra is especially powerful to repeat as you are going to sleep. It seeps into your subconscious to help expedite peace of mind.

Choose a mantra carefully. You can pick a modern mantra or an ancient one. (Research mantras online to find the right one for you.)

Use Your Creativity to Connect

Creativity connects us to the deeper part of ourselves. So it's no surprise that any kind of creativity is a great way to connect us to our loved ones. It opens up our inner world and helps to heal our grief because it throws us into the moment, immersing us in something positive.

If you have ever focused hard on creating a drawing, painting, pottery, sculpture, a woodworking or gardening project—anything that requires creative focus—then you will be familiar with losing track of time.

You are in the moment, and you forget to worry. In fact, when you stop and look up, you might feel stressed about not feeling more stressed out. It's become such a natural state to worry about the future and feel anxiety.

The lack of stress involved in a creative project is so good for you. In a way, it's like an internal massage for the soul. Some say creativity is divine guidance. However you perceive it, the creative process makes us feel alive and tapped into our powerful, positive energy.

Writing is one of the best and most easily accessible creative activities. It helps to create positive thoughts and lifts your energetic vibration. I know the idea of writing can be scary. But *any* kind of writing works.

We've already discussed the "timed write" in Chapter 4 as an action to take for moving through grief; it's a great one for just getting the pen moving across that blank piece of paper. Try this technique to get going, either writing in total silence or to a favorite piece of instrumental music.

It really doesn't matter whether it's a simple gratitude journal, where you list what you're grateful for each night before you go to bed; an ongoing diary of your thoughts and experiences; letters to your loved one; or writing a book. Writing expands awareness and can amplify loving, upbeat energy within you. Remember, Spirit is attracted to that kind of energy.

My client Maria Pe (one of my "Sitter Stories") started journal writing immediately after the devastating murders of her children. It doesn't get much worse for a mother than to go through that. But Pe found a way to get moving with the writing. And in the end, she found writing so healing that she created a book, *Journey to the Upper Realm.* Now, she constantly gets messages from her sons through her writing.

Another client, Father Mark Stuart, wrote a book called *Transforming Grief.* The process of writing the book transformed his own grief and has helped him connect with his partner. But you don't have to become an author to find healing through writing. Anyone can do it.

As well as a notebook, you can write letters to your loved one and keep them in a special box. You might start a blog about your loved one—your memories, your experiences with loss, and connecting with them on the Other Side.

Draw, dance, sing, and write. Create, create, create. Think up some new approaches—you may have a talent or hobby that would be a perfect way for you to open up. Free-associate, think outside the normal approaches, and know there is no "normal" when it comes to creativity.

REMEMBER. When we connect to our creative energy, we're connecting to our inner self, which in turn opens us up to receiving messages from the Other Side. Our loved ones are waiting to connect with us! Help them along with your creativity. And by being creative, we can find our way to peace of mind.

Dream of Them

One of the main ways to receive messages from our loved ones is through our dreams.

Wait, what? Tim, are you saying I can just flick on a dream about my loved one whenever I feel like it? How does that work?

We assume that dreams are completely out of our control, but that is not so.

Dreams are both healing and powerful connectors. They're often called "visitation dreams," where the person who has crossed over comes to us. These may feel different than regular dreams.

When you sleep you are in your subconscious state, which makes you automatically more open and receptive to Spirit. When you are awake, you are more likely to dismiss any signs and messages because your "surface mind" takes control, making you more skeptical.

There are many ways to help ensure a visitation through a dream, from meditation and setting intentions to talking to your loved one right before you go to sleep. If you do this, you will place the thought into your subconscious mind, thus keeping you open and helping you to recall their visit.

On your computer desktop, you might drag a file into a folder. It's the same mental approach with thoughts and dreams. Just set your intention: *Tonight I'm going to dream about this.*

Many of my clients have stories about their loved ones visiting them in their dreams. Don Ruetz (a "Sitter Story") has had a lot of dreams about his sons. Here are two powerful dreams he had recently.

> "I dreamt that I saw my son Jack sitting on a beach. His hair was long in front, partially covering the front of his face. He hugged me, and he was wet and his body was very cold. He said to me, 'I love you. I need you.' I woke

up. This dream was so real when I experienced it. I remember feeling Jack's cold, wet body in this dream.

I had another dream with Jack, where it was a visitation. It was in color, and I saw him face to face really clear. Both dreams made me feel that my son was with me. And that gave me such a sense of peace."

Here are some ideas for how to connect with your dreams:

- **Meditate** on your loved one just before you go to sleep, and set the intention that you will remember your dream. Look at their picture or a special memento of theirs to help set the intention.

- **Talk to your loved one** just as you close your eyes. Again, set the intention and ask for them to come visit you in your dreams. Focus on the love you have for them and ask them to come visit you.

- **Keep a dream journal/notebook at your bedside**. Jot down details of your vivid dreams, especially when your loved one visits. Dreams are powerful connectors and can help with healing our grief. They can be filled with messages, signs, and images of your loved one. So start dreaming and remembering!

Music to Their Ears
(… and Yours)

Music is the universal language. There are more stories than we can count about music uniting cultures, bringing people together who would otherwise not be able to understand each other.

It works on a level of connection unlike any other form of art. It stirs our emotions, colors our stories, and even defines our identities.

No wonder it's a powerful connector to the Other Side. Music not only connects us to each other; it connects us to ourselves.

Everyone has a special piece of music or a personal song they love. Your loved one did, too. Listen to their songs. When you do, you're creating connections and sending them loving energy.

If you happen to have their iPod or their collection of CDs, that's even better. Play them over and over. Not only are you connecting but playing their music can also help with your own healing.

When I gave one of my clients the message to listen to her loved one's music, she finally started listening. Not only was it healing, it turned out she got a wonderful message through the lyrics of one of the songs on his iPod. She felt his presence for the first time since he crossed over. Music can be a powerful connector for you and your loved ones, too.

Here are some ways music can help you connect:

- Listen to your loved one's favorite music (put it on your iPod or other music player). Feel the music. Think of them. Meditate on them. Go for a walk along their favorite path while listening with headphones. Play songs that remind you of your loved one (especially if you don't know their favorite songs), or use your intuition about which songs they would love.

- Randomly press play and listen to the words of the song. It's incredible how relevant the lyrics can be. Remember that signs and messages are everywhere… but you've got to listen.

Let Your Garden Grow

A garden gives us a visceral experience of the circle of life. Gardening helps us to feel good and to "grow" positive thoughts and feelings, which is exactly what we need to do when attempting to open the door to the Other Side.

But, Tim, I'm in grief, and that's about as heavy as energy can get.

That's exactly why this group of activities will help you so much. When we can create positive energy, we're creating more of a chance to connect with our loved one.

You don't need to have a giant backyard to grow a little plant. A balcony is great!

Indoors, you can always have houseplants. It's the *process* of nurturing a plant and watering it that can bring healing energy to your life. Think about it: you're giving life instead of focusing on death.

You go out to your garden and water your hibiscus plant. The next day, a gorgeous pink flower in full bloom is there to greet you. It's like magic! You instantly feel good and can't help but smile in the midst of your sadness. It is so often the *simplest* things that make us feel so good.

By giving life to just one plant, you can create a bond—the plant needs you to water and care for it, and in turn you are getting nurtured and healed by its energy as it grows and thrives. This process gives us a clear reminder that life does go on. While people and other living things pass on, there is a rejuvenation happening at the same time. It's important to find ways to partake in the newness of life as we mourn and remember. Here are some ways to actively participate in the circle of life:

Buy a special plant for you to remember your loved one and nurture it (ideally a plant they loved).

Talk to your loved one as you water your plant and tend your garden. Think of this as nature meditation.

Get out in nature. Go for a hike or a walk. Do something in nature that your loved one would have enjoyed doing with you. Keep thinking of them in loving, positive ways.

REMEMBER—life is energy. Keep vibrant and vital to stay connected. You can't help but feel the connection, especially if a hummingbird shows up!

Follow the Signs and Messages

Signs and messages can pop up anywhere and everywhere. You may end up seeing a lot of them, especially in the first three months after your loved one's passing. My clients often tell me this.

Accept them—do not dismiss them. We don't know when these signs may be from our loved ones. We may never know. It doesn't matter. What matters is to take a leap of faith and allow the sign to be that special message. Just keep your eyes, ears, and senses open!

A client of mine had lost her brother, whom she adored and who was one of her best friends. One day she was in the checkout line at a local food store. On the register display near the Ginger Mints stood a greeting card all by itself. She noticed the beautiful nature setting on the card—mountains, a roaring river, and a giant rainbow.

Suddenly, she had this urge to buy the card and didn't know why. She wasn't even thinking about her brother at the time; she just had this huge desire to purchase the card. When she got home and looked at it again, she realized it was the perfect card for her brother. He loved the mountains more than anything. She put it in her windowsill to remember him.

A few days later, she was talking to her brother while she was running, asking for his guidance. When she got home, the card had fallen into the sink. She dismissed it as the wind knocking it over, but when she checked a little more closely, the window was shut tight. There was no explanation for the card falling.

The next day, it happened again. This time, she stopped and paid attention, taking a leap of faith that it was a sign from him.

A few weeks later, when she was on her computer, suddenly a song title popped up on her screen from iTunes. It was Dan Fogelberg's "Missing You." It came up again and again that day. She had recently bought the song but had never seen that happen. Then she realized it was a message from her brother.

Again, she opened herself to the sign, which made her feel more connected to him and more at peace. She knew he was with her.

The more you open yourself, the more these signs will appear, and the easier it will be to "connect the dots" and realize that they are beyond coincidence. It's really a beautiful messaging system—much more fun and meaningful than texting!

Here are some ways to follow the signs and messages:

- When a sign appears, don't dismiss it. Stop and pay attention.

- Keep a "signs and messages notebook." When you see or get a sign or a message, jot down where and when it happens and when it recurs.

- When you see a sign or message, immediately think of your loved one. Talk to them. Thank them for connecting.

Remember, your loved ones *want* to communicate with you, but you have to learn to read the signs and receive the messages. By actively receiving the messages, you are "giving them the okay" that this channel is open and appreciated. The more you pay attention, the more signs and messages you will receive.

When you tap into your intuition, find that loving feeling, meditate to communicate, listen to their music, write to them, create for them, dream about them, grow a garden, and follow the signs, you'll start to feel more and more connected to yourself and your loved one.

It's then that you can find the healing you are seeking, and maybe along the way your loved one will "stop by for a visit."

7

The Sittings:
Process and Parents

These chapters deal with different types of loss: loss of a parent, loss of a child, loss of a sibling, and so on. Hopefully you can find an example of a situation or circumstance that relates closely to your own experience. The sittings are all very different and really require little or no explanation; they speak for themselves.

This journey I've been on as a medium has taken me down so many roads and along one giant path. I've done 13,000 sittings (and counting) with people from all walks of life—mothers, fathers, sisters, brothers, daughters, sons, police chiefs, doctors, attorneys, directors, actors, writers, professional athletes, business owners, housewives, politicians, designers, celebrities, builders, even priests, and so many others.

Each sitting is as different as the people sitting across from me. But they all have one thing in common: a need to connect and heal after losing their loved one. I've found that through connecting with their loved ones, many people have been able to find healing, peace, and a way to carry on with their lives. Some have used this experience to do wonderful, meaningful work. It's as if their loved ones are guiding them from the Other Side in ways they never imagined.

This is why I do what I do, why I'm excited every day to get up and go to work.

I'm so grateful to be part of this amazing path of connection. I feel it's important to hear the story of my clients' sittings directly from them, so I invited several of my sitters to share their experiences.

Tune in to the experiences of these people and allow their stories to comfort you in the knowledge that all of their loved ones are able to connect with joy and bring the loved ones on this side to closure.

This chapter explains my process, while the subsequent chapters present the sittings themselves.

My Process

Every medium's process is different, yet we all have the same goal: to connect with Spirit—those who've "crossed over"—and then decipher and translate the messages for the loved ones left behind.

I call them "sittings" instead of "readings," because that's what we do: we sit and wait for spirit to come through. So, I'm essentially the middleman.

The rest is left up to you (the sitter) and your loved ones on the Other Side who give messages to me. They are the ones I really work for.

I never know what's going to happen at any given sitting. I don't know who will come through, what they'll say, or if it will make any sense to the sitter (or to me). My job is to let go, be open, trust, and allow Spirit to do its thing.

Preparing to Connect

Everything is pretty straightforward and simple with my process, so there is little preparation. It's all about being in the moment during the sitting.

I begin with a simple mind-clearing meditation. Then I do a lot of breathing, fill my heart with love, and am open to receive. I sit quietly in a peaceful room, with my Buddha fountain in the background, and see what comes through.

For me, the most important part of the process involves paying attention to thoughts and intentions. Just like on this side, our thoughts create our reality. So I have to make sure I am in the headspace where I can be aware of these thoughts.

When we use the power of the mind and the heart, we can connect. Before we begin, I ask my clients to invite whoever it is they wish to contact. I also have the sitter meditate on their loved one beforehand. What we often overlook is the fact that Spirit *wants* to connect with us, and the best way is by being in a loving place with ourselves. It's all very simple. When we realize that, extraordinary experiences can happen.

If I surrender and trust, I'm able to do my job. I have no control over which spirits will connect during a session. I just have to remain open and clear the way so they can connect.

Imagine a translator. When the messages come through, I listen and then share the information. It's the only time when I completely hand over control (and it's not easy for a control freak like me).

Since I never know who is sitting across from me, I don't know who the spirit from the Other Side is either. Sometimes strange messages come through, but I deliver them anyway. At times they don't make sense, or they're a little odd and embarrassing for the client. These are private messages, and as a professional it's not my place to analyze them. I separate myself from the conversation and act only as "the messenger."

The Sitting

As I mentioned, I call these sessions "sittings" instead of "readings," because that's what we do: we sit and wait for Spirit to come through.

During a sitting, I use seeing, hearing, and feeling to receive the messages, so most of the time I'm not even looking at my client; I just tap into the energy of whoever is coming through. I'm looking over their left shoulder or their right shoulder, I'm looking directly behind them or I'm looking into the air directly above them.

When I have sittings with my clients, I only ask for their first name and their telephone number. I neither need nor want to know their last name or any other detailed information about them. The less I know, the better. I like to work knowing that what I am getting from Spirit are true details that only the person in front of me knows. This is essential in the sittings in order to achieve the validation for the sitter that the spirit is indeed their loved one who I'm hearing or seeing. I like to eliminate the static of trust issues so that we can get down to the real reason they are here: to communicate and heal.

Phone Sittings

Whether I do the sitting in person or over the phone, I need to be able to focus without any distractions such as televisions, computers, or ringtones. Sometimes the distractions come from a pushy spirit. (Yeah, they can have human traits like impatience!)

One time, I had a sitter who came early and was waiting in the lobby. I was preparing for the sitting in the room. Suddenly a male spirit came through insisting he needed to talk to her *now*! So I honored his wishes. I went out and pulled her into the session early. Turns out he was her beloved stepfather and a real "life-of-the-party" guy in this life, so on the Other Side he kept that "life of the party" immediate energy going.

No Guarantees

I always let my clients know that there are never any guarantees in a sitting with regards to who comes in and who doesn't.

Sometimes, it's very disheartening when a client has flown in from out of the country to come and see me, and her deceased husband does not come in, but instead her neighbor whom she knew when she was growing up comes in very strongly.

That's the hard part of doing this work—seeing disappointment in the sitter. It does not happen that often, but it does happen. It could be that the spirit trying to come through doesn't create the energy needed for me to see them. We can't dwell on the spirits that don't show up. I always press on and see what messages come through anyway.

What is relayed to me is usually delivered through the spirit that is coming in the strongest.

An Average Sitting

Let me describe an average sitting. To begin, we sit facing one another. I don't make small talk. I just get right to work.

Guided Meditation

First, I let them know that I will be doing an opening meditation. This is a two- to three-minute guided meditation where I run the energy through the seven chakras of our bodies.

I do this to clear out both myself and the client, in order to make us feel much more relaxed and comfortable. I can forget about my previous sittings that day, and my client can forget about the long drive or plane ride they took to come and have the sitting with me. I also find that it makes Spirit much more comfortable when we begin with this meditation.

Organizing Clutter

Next, I always explain to my client that when I look over their left shoulder, I am seeing a spirit from their mother's side of the family. When I look over their right shoulder, it's a spirit from their father's side of the family. When I look directly behind them, this tells me that this is the spirit of a husband/wife, brother/sister, son/daughter, cousin, or friend.

Sometimes I will be doing a sitting and I will bring in a woman on the mother's side and the client will say, "No, that's on my dad's side." I will be able to look at the client and say they are coming through very clearly on the mother's side, and after providing more detailed information, the client will agree and say, "Oh! That is my mom's mom."

Not all mediums work in this manner. This is my way of "organizing clutter."

"Not Bothered"

People in a sitting might ask, "Aren't we bothering them? What if they're trying to rest in peace?" The truth is, Spirit wants to make contact in most cases. They want their family and loved ones to know that they're okay and that they have made it to the Spirit side.

And it doesn't matter how they died. Sometimes Spirit is incredibly upbeat after a horrific death. Like this man recently who had been decapitated. He was laughing and so happy on the Other Side and couldn't wait to connect. So the details of the passing don't always reflect the state of being of each spirit.

Love Is Stronger Than Need

When Spirit wants to come through, it takes energy on their part as well. The mental invitation that is sent is a loving one with intentions of communication. Love is a stronger vibration than need. An invitation shouldn't be of a lower vibration, such as, "I need to talk to you because I need your help, so please come through." Spirit has the free will to come in or not.

Positivity

If the room is filled with an abundance of love as we do this work, those on the Spirit side feed off of that love, and it gives them energy that enables them to come through. The more you understand physics, the more you will understand metaphysics and the belief that thought creates reality.

Thoughts are real. I've found this to be so true in my work. If the sitter is filled with negative thoughts, it can act as a barrier against connecting. For example, a man dies, leaving his wife to mourn. She lingers in a deep depression for months. "I miss him every day. I can't go on without him" is her cry. His spirit is brought down to a lower vibration as a result of her depressive energy, which keeps her from connecting with him on the Other Side.

Look back through Chapter 4 and 5 to work through depressive energy.

Recording

Each sitting is recorded. At the end of the sitting, I encourage the sitter to listen to the session over and over. It's a great way to keep the connection going beyond the sitting, and to keep them open to the signs of their loved one's presence on a daily basis. Often we'll miss the signs because we dismiss them as coincidence or even reject them. Our task is to "wake up" and recognize them.

The thing to remember is, our loved ones aren't really gone, and they're around us. All we have to do is unplug from our overbooked, overworked, over-everything lives for even a moment, "talk" to them, and listen. Then we may begin to fill the tremendous void we have with this newfound energy.

Life can get better.

Sometimes, it is helping the sitter get used to the new normal with the validations that come in from Spirit. It will never be the same without that person in front of us, and though we'll never forget, we can heal.

I feel grateful that I can be the middleman for those trying to connect. It's the best gift I've ever received, and the best one I can give.

I'll finish this introduction to the sittings themselves with one particular experience. As I said, every sitting is as unique as the sitter (and the spirits on the Other Side!). Sometimes there is a powerful breakthrough. Sometimes a sitter will walk in the door in a certain state of mind, and by the time they walk out the door, a transformation has taken place.

One of the challenges to being a medium is the skeptics. Sometimes they can be the ones who surprise themselves and me. Skeptics and mediums seem to go hand in hand, par for the metaphysical course. But sometimes, something amazing and unexpected will happen.

Frank's Story
(The Skeptic)

Helen was elated after her sitting with me, so much so that she came back the next week with her big burly husband, Frank, in tow, who owns a tow truck company.

In one chair sat Helen, all smiles, open and excited to be there, hoping for Frank to have the same wonderful experience as she had had. Frank sat in the other chair, arms folded, lips pursed, looking as if he was in a jury assembly room waiting to be called for a panel.

We began with the usual ritual of a brief meditation, where we sat with our eyes closed, breathing deeply, sending loving thoughts and inviting in departed loved ones. Then I had this urge to peek, so I opened one eye. There was Frank, sitting staring at the wall, arms still folded across his chest, still with "the look" on his face. Classic skeptic. I shut my one eye and took a deep breath. I always love a challenge.

We opened our eyes, and I began the session. Messages started coming through. Frank barely listened, checking his watch every minute or so (at least he didn't storm out of the room). Helen sat forward in her chair, eager for more messages.

I turned to Frank and said, "There's a male behind you. He was shot and killed in Vietnam."

He looked at me sarcastically and said, with his pursed lips and the "prove it to me" look still on his face, "I had lots of friends who died in Vietnam. Which one is it?"

At that moment, his friend on the Other Side put his hand over his testicles and said, "Tell him I got my left testicle shot off."

I turned to Helen (the good Catholic boy in me had to apologize ahead of time). "I hope you're okay with what I'm about to say."

She assured me, "Please go ahead. It's fine." Frank started to sit up in his chair (arms still crossed, though,) now slightly ready to listen.

So I continued, "He says his left testicle was shot off in Vietnam. Does this make sense to you, Frank?"

Frank slowly uncrossed his arms, took a very deep breath, leaned forward, put his head in his hands, and burst into tears. After a few minutes, he was finally able to speak. "Yes, I understand who that is. We were best buddies in Vietnam. He did get his left testicle shot off, but he didn't die there. He died of cancer years later. I always teased him about it—getting his left nut shot off. We would always laugh about it."

The sadness and anger that had been holding Frank down and weighing on his soul was lifted that day. Frank walked out of the room a little lighter, with uncrossed arms and a smile on his face. It's one of my favorite skeptic stories, and that is why I wanted to share it.

But now, I think it's important to hear from the sitters themselves.

We all will lose a loved one at some point in our lives. And we'll all need to find a way to cope, heal, and to hopefully thrive. These people (the sitters) whom I have given messages to from their loved ones are all finding their way after coping with tremendous loss and doing amazing things with their lives. They inspire me to keep going with this work.

What follows are their fascinating stories about their own journeys in connecting with the Other Side.

Losing a Parent

It doesn't matter how old we are, or that our mother or father "had a good, long life," when we lose a parent, we lose a part of our past—the part that has been with us the longest. They were the ones who often loved us unconditionally.

Our parents are our history from the beginning of our lives, whether we had a good relationship with them or not. We expect that they will leave us one day—it's considered a milestone of our adult life—but when it happens, we're never really prepared. When they go, a part of us goes with them, forcing us to be all grown up. We may feel like a child, yearning for our mother or father to protect us and love us unconditionally once again, especially if that parent is our best friend.

Ed Cook's Story

When I lost my mother in 2004, I was really struggling with my grief. Although my mom was older, and of course it's a natural progression of life to eventually lose our parents in later years, it was particularly difficult because she was my best friend. We were soul mates. We spent a lot of time together, taking daily walks, sharing our thoughts, our outlook on life, our feelings about my dad (who was gone). She was my anchor. The world made sense when my mom was here. So when she died, I was beside myself. I felt so lost.

I found out about Tim through my massage therapist; she had a client who went to him. So after my mom died, I made an appointment. As a criminal defense attorney, I deal in evidence, so I was very skeptical at first. I made sure Tim knew nothing about me other than my name.

I came into the session with no expectations—which was probably a good thing. My mind was open to receiving any messages that would come. My mother always encouraged me to be open. Hopefully, she would come through with guidance from the Other Side. I needed desperately to hear from her.

We began with a meditation. This part was familiar because I had been meditating for years. It's always been a great tool to release the intense stress of doing criminal defense work in downtown Los Angeles.

When we opened our eyes and began, Tim immediately said, "Your dad is here."

I wanted to be sure it was him so I asked, "What's his name?"

"Edward. Same as you. He's apologizing for never being able to admit he made a mistake for anything."

I thought, *Now, Tim could not have possibly known about this.* My mom and I would always talk on our walks about Dad never being able to apologize for mistakes. My sister came through, too. ("Your sister is here and says her lungs are fine now.") She had died of lung cancer. I was beginning to think there was something to this mediumship stuff. But I really wanted to hear from my mom.

Then Tim said, "There's a woman claiming to be your mother. Her name is Margaret or Mary. No, wait, she's saying Marion. Her name is Marion."

I could hardly believe it. That was my mother's name! The minute she came through, it was as if all the heavy sadness disappeared and I felt at peace. I just nodded. But on the inside I was jumping up and down for joy. I was still I keeping things close to the vest until I knew this was for real.

Tim continued, "Your mother comes to visit you in your house near the ocean. She walks in the front door, turns right, and sits down at the glass table." This was uncanny! Not only did Tim describe my house, but the glass table was where my mom would always sit and prune my plants.

Now I have this little ritual. Sometimes I'll walk in my front door, immediately turn right, and sit "next to her" at that glass table

I've also had a lot of friends "stop by for a visit." (At my age of seventy-four, someone is always crossing over.) I even had Johnnie Cochran come through several times. Tim said, "There's a JC here. He says his full name is Johnnie Cochran. (JC was my nickname for him. Tim had no idea I was an attorney!) He's saying, 'I see you're still a lawyer, Ed. If you need any help let me know.'" It was definitely Johnnie. We had a lot of history together.

Recently, a friend of mine died, and I went to Tim just a few days after his death. He came right through with specific details. But then Tim saw tubes connected to him in the hospital. I thought, *Tim wasn't right on this one*. So that night I called his wife. Turns out my friend indeed had tubes connected to him!

At another sitting with Tim, my mom came through with information that ended up saving my life. After my wife and I came back from the Galapagos Islands, I woke up every morning coughing. I went to the doctor and had a chest X-ray and everything was fine. But the coughing continued, so I ended up getting a spit test. It turned out I had a virulent fungus in my chest. I attributed it to our Galapagos trip. Around that time, I had a session with Tim and my mom came through. I asked her about the fungus, and why I was still coughing. She said it was mold in my house. I called the mold extractors, and sure enough that's exactly what it was. There was mold everywhere. We even had to move out of our house for several weeks. After the mold was removed, my coughing stopped and I was much better. The mold extractors told me that if I hadn't removed the mold it could have killed me. I would have never thought about the mold being the cause if my mom hadn't come through to tell me. So I have my mom (and Tim) to thank for saving my life. That sitting has been the most important of all the sittings after ten years of going to Tim.

This whole experience with Tim expedited the grieving process with my mom so I could get on with my life. I feel her presence all the time. Her parting words when she knew she was dying were, 'I'm never going to leave you, Ed.' Turns out she held true to her promise.

Having the connection with our parent in Spirit can give us a sense of peace and comfort. We may even feel protected in a brand new way.

The sitters' stories and the messages from their loved ones are the cornerstone of what I do. Each one is so different, fascinating, and meaningful. They are like a window opening into the mystery of life. And, just like each person's journey is uniquely his or hers, each passing is as well. It's through sharing their stories of grief, healing, and connection that we can perhaps understand a little more about the circle of life.

8

The Sittings:
Children and Family

When a loved one transitions suddenly, the reaction is more severe for those on this side. Our very preconceptions about life and "what should have been" can be shaken to the core, adding another element to the grieving process.

Those who have experienced this find an extra degree of comfort in connecting with their loved ones after an unexpected transition.

Losing a Sibling

Losing a sibling has its special challenges because it is not often considered as painful a loss as losing a child or a spouse. The sibling left behind can feel left out because of this.

When a parent loses a child, or a spouse loses their husband or wife, there is tremendous focus and support, as family and friends rally around them in their time of grief. But siblings can be left alone with their grief. Society doesn't see it as such a huge loss.

And if a person is especially close to their lost brother or sister, the pain can be unbearable. It's like a piece of them has been yanked away, like a missing limb. It becomes part of the sibling's history that is now just that—history.

If the sibling was the older brother or sister, they may have been like a father or mother to the ones left behind. There is a certain loss of emotional security.

And when the sibling takes his or her own life without any forewarning, it's a pain unlike any other. It becomes a double whammy—losing a loved one and then coping with the way they died.

But when we connect with them in Spirit, through a message or, in this story, a song, it can be a powerful guide to the healing we need.

In September 2010, Tracy Pattin lost her beloved brother very suddenly. After thirty years as a paraplegic, he needed to get out of his body. He had taken his own life.

Tracy Pattin's Story

I meditated that morning, getting ready for my sitting with Tim. I sent love to my brother and asked him to connect with me during the session. It had been six months since he died, and I missed him terribly. He was so important in my life. We were important to each other. He was one of my best friends, my guide, and my champion. The one who made life make sense. I always felt he knew something the rest of us didn't.

He had been in a wheelchair for thirty years after a bad fall, and had had enough. So one day he went to the mountains, the place he loved to be more than anywhere, and he took his life. The day I got the news, my life came to a screeching halt. Everything looked so different. I was in this strange new reality. When I looked to the future, it was dark and dreary, like a foggy, rainy day that never ends.

When I walked into the room for the sitting with Tim, there was a small group of eight people waiting for our Spirit Circle. I wondered, what were their stories? How did they cope with their loss? Suddenly, I didn't feel so alone. We were all there to connect with our loved ones. I held my brother's Peace Dollar, which was with him when he died, tight in my palm and prayed for a message.

Tim scanned the room, stopping at different sitters to deliver a message. There would be a brief back and forth as Tim delivered the message. Then the sitter would smile, understanding the message and nodding that it was their loved one coming through. I kept hoping Tim would stop at me.

Finally, Tim looked at me. "I see a male standing behind you." He went on to describe various details. My brother was giving me a "thumbs up" for the projects I was working on. (I could just see him doing that. He always rooted for me.) Then Tim said, "He's saying he wants you to listen to his music. It was very important to him, and it's important for you. Do you understand this?"

I started to cry. I knew exactly what it meant. My brother loved music, almost more than anything. The one thing I requested from the family after he died was his iPod. When I would visit him in northern California, we used to listen to it in the car as we would drive around, talking excitedly about our hopes and dreams. He'd always play something from his 2,000 songs that I'd never heard or some oldie that brought back a host of memories. But I hadn't listened to it. I couldn't. Not yet.

Tim's message from my brother stayed with me for a year, haunting me. The scratched silver iPod sat in the drawer, waiting. Occasionally I'd look at it and touch it. But, I just couldn't press Play. I wasn't ready—until recently, on another year anniversary of his death.

I decided to make this year different. So I invited a small group of friends over to celebrate his life—and to finally play his music. It was a huge step, but it was time. So I charged it up (even that was emotional—besides, what if it didn't activate?). My friend brought over little speakers. We all gathered around. I decided the first random song to play would be his message to me. My heart was beating fast waiting to hear what would come on—what this message would be.

It was a simple guitar playing the most beautiful, gentle song that I'd never heard before. At first I was disappointed that someone wasn't singing "his message" to me. But then I surrendered to it, knowing it was the right song. I looked at the name. The album was

"Look Out For Hope" and the song was "In the Sweet By and By" (by S. Fillmore Bennett and Joseph P. Webster). I found the lyrics and started to read as we listened:

> *There's a land that is fairer than day,*
> *And by faith we can see it afar;*
> *For the Father waits over the way*
> *To prepare us a dwelling place there.*
> *In the sweet by and by,*
> *We shall meet on that beautiful shore;*
> *In the sweet by and by,*
> *We shall meet on that beautiful shore.*
>
> *We shall sing on that beautiful shore*
> *The melodious songs of the blessed;*
> *And our spirits shall sorrow no more,*
> *Not a sigh for the blessing of rest.*
> *To our bountiful Father above,*
> *We will offer our tribute of praise*
> *For the glorious gift of His love*
> *And the blessings that hallow our days.*

It was the perfect song. I felt like he was right there with me. I was so grateful to Tim for giving me the message from my brother to listen. Only one other person at my gathering had ever met my amazing brother. But I think they all met him that night.

If we can keep the memories alive through things like music, there can be ways to have a new relationship with that brother or sister, now in Spirit.

Losing a Child

It's probably the worst kind of loss to experience. An unimaginable nightmare. In the cycle of life, parents aren't supposed to bury their children.

There is a tremendous amount of anger, guilt, and depression that comes with this loss. Marital problems can reemerge or develop because of the immense stress on each parent as they struggle to cope with this horrible new reality. They may even separate and divorce because of their child's death.

Parents seek all kinds of support, from family therapy to support groups to writing a journal, and some seek out a medium to reach out to their child in Spirit.

I have had so many parents come to me desperately wanting to connect with their deceased child (and in some cases, children)—not just because they miss them but also because they're desperate to know if they're alright.

It turns out that often not only are the children okay but they're thriving on the Other Side, eager to protect their parents on this side.

And most of them come through very clearly. What was a horrific tragedy transforms into powerful healing and even peaceful bliss for the parents.

On Tuesday, June 21, 2011, in San Diego, California, Maria Pe's life would change in the most horrific, tragic way imaginable. Her sons were murdered... by their father.

Maria Pe's Story

Tuesday, June 21, 2011. It was a normal morning for me. I had just finished getting ready for work and was about to head to my office. I went to click the TV off when a news story caught my attention: "Murder-Suicide in Bonita." The camera panned to a familiar neighborhood. I saw the house across the street from my ex-husband Tom's house. My heart began to beat faster. Panic set in. The news reporter said a man and two young boys had been killed. I knew it was my sons. My ex-husband had killed Sean (fifteen) and Kyle (thirteen). He had given them sleeping pills to put them in a deep sleep, then shot them in their own beds. Then my ex-husband shot himself.

I have never felt such depths of despair. I didn't think this type of pain and anguish could be possible. I wondered if my physical body could survive it. Sometimes when I wake up in the middle of the night, I see images of the boys in their beautiful human forms and then I start envisioning the horror of their death. The pain is so intense it gnaws at my being, leaving me feeling so empty, lost, and alone. It's so hard to be here, to be alive, when my boys are somewhere else. I needed to connect with them.

This was my first hour-long session with a medium, so I was nervous and anxious, and a bit skeptical (the attorney in me). But I was open to the experience. I sat with Tim, and we did a brief meditation, which helped to calm me. I was a little afraid the boys weren't going to come through. I wanted to know if what I was experiencing in my own "journey meditations," where I connected with my sons, was real. I needed an objective validation of their continued existence, so this sitting was critical. My sons had promised me in one of my meditations earlier in the week that they would come through. They were the ones who picked Tim after I considered several other mediums.

Tim was quiet for a moment. I could tell something was happening. Then he looked behind my shoulder and said, "I see a young male standing behind you." When Tim said that a young male was waving and trying to get his attention, I knew it was Kyle. It was exactly what he would do. Then he said, "Do you have a picture of your son in your wallet when he was seven years old?" I couldn't believe he knew that. I'd been carrying his picture for a few months now. I didn't normally carry any photos in my wallet! My brother had given me an older picture of my sons in November, and I had just put it in my wallet.

Then Tim asked, "What's this about Red Vines licorice? Does this make sense to you?" Again, I could hardly believe what I was hearing. It made total sense. Kyle loved red licorice. He was constantly eating Red Vines. Tim also said Kyle was a world traveler. Totally on point! He was only thirteen, but he had already traveled across the globe.

Tim continued, "There's another male coming through. He says he's sorry that he's running late." It had to be Sean. He ran late a lot. Then Tim started to give more little details that he couldn't possibly know, but I did. "He is showing me that he loves Cool Ranch Doritos. He's eating the chips and cracking them in my ear to get attention away from your younger son. Does that make sense?"

It made sense and made me laugh. This is exactly how Sean operated. He would not have jumped up and down to get attention; he was a lot subtler, and very funny about how he did things. It was another characteristic that gave me confirmation of Sean's presence.

Then Tim started to describe what happened on that horrible day. "Was it a bullet that took him over? I feel like there was a gun going off and, *bam*, he's gone. He was sleeping when this happened. Is that right? He says he went to sleep and woke up on Spirit side. The fifteen-year-old. He was also shot, is that right?"

It was all so accurate. At first I was shocked Tim knew it was a bullet. As he described what had happened, I began to cry hard. It was painful and emotional, but also validating and somehow a relief. And I was thankful to hear that they had felt no pain, that they had been sleeping and crossed over to the Spirit side in their sleep. And it resonated strongly with me when Kyle talked about the emotional pain I went through after their deaths. It was as if they had seen me at the time I arrived at the house, when the police officers told me what had happened.

Then Tim asked, "Did their father do this?" Tim explained how children who passed over at or around the same time as a parent were usually with that parent on Spirit side, but not in this case. Tim did not see their father.

The boys conveyed to Tim that they were not around him, that he was in a different place, kind of like a timeout or confinement, and that they were both very okay with it. Tim said the boys were conveying that there was nothing I could have done to prevent what had happened and that I should not feel responsible. Then the boys said, "We're not angry at Dad. We forgive him."

During my second reading with Tim, both boys came through immediately. Tim said, "The boys said last night around 8:30 they knew you were talking to them, wanting them to come here today." At first I was caught off guard, but then I remembered that I *was* "talking" to them the night before about coming to the session. Then Tim saw the boys with a birthday cake for me. My birthday was two weeks away.

The boys went on to talk about their names being read over a loudspeaker at an event and that they knew the community had come together. Tim said, "Both of them are showing me so clearly how their passing touched so many lives, and they're thanking literally hundreds of people." Then the boys said, "We're not angry at Dad. We forgive him. Now it's your turn."

After the tragedy, I started to write. It helped me to process my grief, and it gave me a sense of peace, so I started writing every day. It became a journal and then it turned into a book. I am sharing it to help others.

I'm not just trying to get over a loss. There is no "getting over" something like this. But I'm trying to learn and grow from it. And another way I've been able to heal is through the people who have been there for me. I've been so blessed in my life with people who are willing to take this journey with me. This is one of the reasons I've been able to keep going.

I know I'm supposed to be enjoying life on Earth now. I've found a way to be happy again because my sons showed me what life is all about—learning to love better and to choose love over fear. I know that when I transition I will have accomplished what I needed to accomplish. Tim said that they hear me when I talk to them.

My sitting with Tim was the objective validation I needed. It was a big turning point for me and a major change in how I view the world and the afterlife. I see death very differently now. I'm not afraid of it. The souls live on. Although I feel sad for the people left behind, I understand that the souls have done what they came here for.

I asked my boys on the Other Side, "How do I make a difference and live a meaningful life?"

They said to me, "One person at a time, Mom. One person at a time."

Here is Maria's dedication to her sons (from her book, *Journey to the Upper Realm: How I Survived the Deaths of My Sons and Learned to Communicate with Them on the Other Side*):

For Sean and Kyle:
The lights of my life and my greatest teachers.
All that time I thought I was teaching you.
And you were really here to teach me.
I honor you.

Loss of Entire Family:
Don Ruetz's Story

On July 16, 2005, in the blink of an eye, Don Ruetz lost his entire immediate family in a plane crash.

Everything changed in the most drastic way imaginable in the early morning of July 16, 2005. My entire family—my wife Cynthia and sons Jack and Justin, along with their friend Connor and his father, Paul (who was my good friend), died in a plane crash as they were touring Playa Domingo in Costa Rica. I was nearby at our home when it happened.

After the funeral in California, I flew back to Costa Rica. As I was driving from the airport to our home in Playa Flamingo, the harsh reality set in—my family would not be there to greet me. The kids and I would not go surfing; my wife and I would not have dinner at our favorite restaurant, sipping margaritas as we watched the waves. I was totally alone.

Now, I desperately needed to know where they were. What happened to them? Were their spirits around me? Being a former police officer for thirty years, I didn't believe in that sort of thing. We were always about the facts. But now, I was open. So I called Tim to make an appointment.

At the sitting, my wife Cynthia and my sons Justin and Jake showed up with personal messages, details only I would know.

Cynthia came through with a message saying, "Thank you for what you did for the boys." I had set up special plaques with their names on it. Then she said, "Tell him I've been with him at the Catalinas (where their plane crashed). When you go to the cliff and sit by yourself, I'm with you and so are the kids." There was no way Tim would have known about that. I couldn't believe it. Then Cynthia talked about Hawaii and us going to the Big Island, which we'd done. Suddenly, I felt like she was right next to me. I wasn't so alone anymore.

Then Tim saw Justin with a birthday cake for me. He placed it on my lap. It was my birthday. Tim told me he was kissing me, saying, "My dad taught me how to give affection." Justin and I would always talk about showing affection. It was like a scene from my life when they were alive.

Then my son Jack came through. He was telling me about something he'd seen me doing recently. "You pick up this object and rub it." Tim said it was like a picture frame. It was uncanny. I had a daily routine of rubbing my fingers over the lips of my two boys on a caricature of Justin and Jack done at Disneyland. Their caricatures sat inside a picture frame outside the door to my bedroom. Each night before bedtime, I would place my fingers on their lips in the photo as a nightly kiss.

Since this tragedy, I've been to Tim several times. This experience has taught me that we're predestined in this life. This helped me in my healing process and gave me the motivation to go on to accomplish so many things. I built a yoga center commemorating my wife and a basketball court in memory of Jack and Justin.

Not only do I feel connected to my family, it's like we have a new relationship in Spirit. From the Other Side, they inspire me to move on with my life and make contributions to my Costa Rican community. They're my champions, my guides, and still my family.

9

The Sittings:
Everlasting Connections

Finding that our loved ones not only continue to exist on the Other Side, but are able to connect with us is an amazing dimension to the whole experience.

Losing a Spouse or
Longtime Companion

Although a parent losing a child is excruciating beyond comprehension, losing a spouse or longtime companion is like having our legs cut off at the knees, leaving the loved one left behind so empty, so lost.

They have lived with this person day in and day out. The memories are everywhere and there is no easy way to escape them. Going home to a silent, empty house can be daunting. The realization of being alone acts like salt in the wound. Life has changed dramatically. Nothing looks or feels the same, from the empty side of the bed to being left now with just the memories of that person. The spouse or companion has to reinvent himself or herself, find a new way to live their lives.

No one can get around this feeling, even if you're a priest, filled with faith and understanding of life's mysteries.

Mark Stuart is an Episcopal priest who lost his best friend, companion, and life partner of twelve years on a pilgrimage to the Holy Land. Here's his story: (taken from his book, *Transforming Grief*).

As a side note: I had lost contact with Mark and had no way of reaching him for this story. When I set the intention to find him, the very next day, at one of my Sittings, the Sitter told me after the session that this wonderful priest, Father Mark Stuart, had recommended me!

The Universe works in amazing ways.

Father Mark Stuart

On January 21, 2009, my life as I knew it ended. My dear Bob died of a hematoma brain hemorrhage while we were on our trip to Israel. I never felt such loneliness, isolation, sadness, and despair. Six months earlier, my mother had died. She was eighty-five years old and lived a good, full life. Her passing did not prepare me at all for this experience. Losing a parent is like losing a part of your past; losing your spouse is losing not only part of your past, but also both your present and your future.

Being an Episcopal priest didn't make this any easier, as it challenged my faith's position on life after death. This experience would open me up to explore a world beyond the physical life. Bob was only forty-one years old when he left this life, less than half my mom's age. He was sixteen years younger than I, and I always assumed he would be surviving me. I entered a very dark time when I lost him. In fact, I do not remember much of those first weeks following his death. What I do remember are vignettes of searing pain and bitter tears.

By the time summer had arrived and I had continued my readings on grief, life after death, and after-death communication, I became more and more drawn to the idea of seeking out a medium. So I went on a search to find the right one for me. One day I was searching on the Internet and a name just popped up: Tim Braun. I had a good feeling about his website, so I called and made an appointment.

My mother came through right away. She was thanking me for being so much a part of her life. She had a lot to say, but I was really anxious to hear from Bob. All of a sudden, Tim said, "Do you know why she's talking about B-O-B? (She was spelling out the name to Tim.) She says, 'Tell Mark I'm all around Bob.'" She just kept repeating this message to Tim.

Then Tim said, "Bob is looking at you and says, 'I never got to say goodbye to him.' He shows me that there was no closure, but he's snapping his fingers, explaining that he went quickly and there was no pain."

I listened to the tape all the way home in the car. I was giddy and crying at the same time. I was able to connect to Bob (and myself) on a level I had never experienced. What I used to believe I now know.

I ended up sharing my journey of the first year, including the session with Tim, in my book, *Transforming Grief*. Prior to publication, I asked my bishop for his blessing, which he hardly ever gave, and he said, "Mark, you need to publish the book."

This whole experience, from losing my beloved Bob to connecting with him in the afterlife, has taught me that life is a tapestry. And with every experience, no matter how painful, we add a new weft to that tapestry—a new chapter to our lives. As we feel their energy "across the veil," and if we open our hearts to their guidance, we can do great things—perhaps things we never imagined, just as we never imagined having to deal with the overwhelming loss and grief.

When a spouse/longtime companion is able to connect with their loved one on the Other Side, it can be like a new lease on life for them. Although they will always miss that person and never stop loving them, getting a message from them, knowing they're there in Spirit can help the loved one left behind navigate this challenging new reality.

Loss in Wartime:
Tony and Carol's Story

In January 2004, Tony and Carol DiRaimondo lost their son Michael in Iraq. Michael was a flight medic. He was killed, along with three other crewmembers and five patients, when a missile hit their helicopter.

Tony said: "Losing your child is not something that you prepare for. It was more painful for us because Michael was due to come home in eight weeks. You want to live with the belief that medics are the most protected of all in the service. But sadly, that wasn't the case that day."

Tony

I never thought I would be going to a medium. I'm the biggest skeptic there is. Prior to my son's passing, I was a solid believer that once you're dead, you're dead. That's it. I didn't believe there was life beyond life. I never considered that there was anything more.

But when we lost Michael, everything changed. My world was so devastated that I opened up to the possibility. I was willing to listen, to connect with his spirit. During several sittings, Tim gave us messages—specific information that was beyond what anybody could possibly know. It was a gift.

My wife and I took a Mediterranean cruise last year. When we went to see Tim shortly after we returned (Tim had no idea we had been to Italy). Michael came through excited about our trip and said, "It's about time you took a cruise. Didn't you have a great time in Italy?" It was one more validation that Michael was there in Italy with us.

Another time, we had just come back from a trip to Hawaii with our family. When we went to Tim, the first thing he said was, "Michael is putting Hawaiian leis around both of your necks, and he's saying, 'Wasn't it a great trip?' Then Tim asked us, "Did you guys just go to Hawaii?" Again, it reinforced our belief that Michael was right there in the room with us.

Then there was the time our granddaughter was visiting. We were playing "Ring Around the Rosie." All of a sudden my granddaughter stops, sticks her hand out and says, "Come on, play!" We asked her who she was talking to. She said, "Uncle Michael! He's right there!" So we left a spot open for Michael in the circle.

There's always something that comes out that reinforces not only our belief in life after death but our knowledge that Michael is still with us. He's still around us all the time. This gives us such a sense of peace. And the sittings with Tim have impacted me in my daily life. I'm more open and aware of the messages and signs from Michael. Before, I would never have looked for them. Now I am so grateful for every one of them.

For me, my son may not be physically with us, but he is with us. And I believe that. I accept it because that's all I'm going to get. I know Michael's not going to walk through the door. I doubt that I'm ever going to have a vision while I'm conscious. But I know Michael is with me all the time. There are always things Tim says in a sitting that he couldn't possibly know. Things that occurred just between my son and me. I became a very solid believer in life beyond life.

Carol

When we lost Michael, I thought I'd never be able to leave the house. But then I started to notice signs that seemed to be connected to Michael. All I wanted to know was that he was okay.

The first message from him was on a license plate on a car in front of me. The personalized license plate read, "I AM OK MA." Unbelievable. If you ask for the signs, you get them. Then I have to thank him. When the signs started showing up everywhere, I knew Michael was here. I wanted to know more.

When we went to Tim, Michael came through immediately and in a big way. (I'm not surprised because he was always so outgoing!) After our annual "Michael birthday" trip this year, we realized Michael was with us the whole time! And he had a hand in upgrading us to a suite! When Tim gave us that message, I knew Michael was with us and would always be. I saw many signs of Michael in Hawaii. I knew in my heart that he wasn't going to miss the all-expenses-paid vacation with the family!

Losing Michael has taught me so much, especially about forgiveness. I can't be angry because somewhere in Iraq there are parents who are grieving over their child. So who will I be angry with? The "why me?" anger was never in the picture.

We can't even begin to thank Tim for his hand in helping us understand that Michael didn't "die" on January 8, 2004; he just entered a new realm. He lives on in all of us. We visit Tim around the hardest times of the year: Christmas and his birthday in June. Our children, sons-in-law, and grandchildren will forever keep in touch with their brother, brother-in-law, and uncle, thanks to Tim. We believe Michael sent Tim to help us cope, and we will forever be grateful.

I have been amazed and so inspired by these parents who have managed to find healing and some sort of peace of mind when they connect with their children in Spirit.

What has been especially powerful and moving is how they have gone on to do meaningful work and help others heal in the midst of dealing with their enormous tragedies.

10

The New Normal

When people are dealing with loss, there is a constant search to make sense of their new reality. Everyone grieves differently, but it's important to deal with our feelings, to feel the sadness, and hopefully again find peace and bliss in our lives. It's rewarding to be a part of this process.

The result often offers a sense of closure for the sitter, and sometimes it can also act as an opening to a new relationship with the person who's no longer here physically.

When a sitter comes in with such a heavy, sad energy and I'm able to help transform that in some way, it's the greatest feeling. This is their gift and Spirit's gift to *me*. And I'm forever grateful. I always say, "I work for Spirit. They're my true employers!" If I can provide an hour or even a moment of peace, then I feel like I've done my job.

The sitters' stories and the messages from their loved ones are the cornerstone of what I do. Each one is so different, fascinating, and meaningful. They are like a window opening into the mystery of life.

Understanding

In the same way that each person's journey is uniquely their own, each passing is unique as well. It's through sharing stories of grief, healing, and connection that we can perhaps understand a little more about the circle of life.

Understanding comes by degrees, a little at a time. It's like climbing a mountain path through fog: we can only see so far ahead, perhaps ten or twenty feet. Without noticing, we can suddenly see thirty feet ahead… then our body begins to cast a shadow. Before we know it, blue sky is above us and we are in clear sunlight. We look around and can see the fog we just walked through is now behind us. We can see the entire mountain range beyond the fogbank. We have an entirely new perspective. Until recently all we knew was fog; now we can see valleys, mountains, forests, sky, and clouds.

In the same way, when we discover an entirely new dimension to life, it can feel as if a veil has been lifted. Knowing there is an Other Side that continues past our life puts everything in perspective.

Coming to light during the grieving process, this experience can create an especially positive new approach to the issue of living. We were not only trapped in the fog; we were lodged deep in a narrow valley. Now we feel free.

For others it may just create more questions, and feel like the beginning of a journey up a bigger mountain in order to learn more. Again, just "knowing" there is more than meets the eye is a small step toward answering our concerns about loved ones who have left us, and "how they are doing." I hope that the sittings provide a certain amount of reassurance, even if you have not yet been able to experience a sitting yourself.

Skeptics

Some people will always be skeptical until they have the experience for themselves. Many of my sitters were initially skeptical. Maria Pe was. So was Frank, and so was Jack in Hawaii.

Skepticism is completely understandable. Until recently, mediums were cast in the category of after-dinner entertainment, along with theatrical magicians and crystal ball–reading mystics. The very idea that a medium could be a scientific practitioner is only just beginning to gain acceptance.

Just like I have to surrender and trust my gift, I have to surrender and trust that the skeptics have their own path. The point is, there are believers and disbelievers, just as there are charlatans and authentic mediums. It's the same as any other industry, or any part of society. There are always people with integrity and people who lack integrity.

I have a gift for connecting with Spirit, just like others have a gift for singing, painting, dancing, writing, and acting and can't explain how. They don't know how they know; they just know they have a gift. Of course, it takes practice to develop that gift. And it's up to them to decide what to do with it.

I have a healthy acceptance of all these points of view, knowing that the world around us is in the process of shifting, moving away from the "flat earth" belief of a three-dimensional world, in which we are "here today, gone tomorrow," toward a wider acceptance of our journey and its spiritual "through-line."

Further Perspectives

By expanding our knowledge of the Other Side, further perspectives become visible. For example, the idea is widely discussed that our time on this plane might be more planned ahead than we initially believe.

If you choose to climb farther up your mountain of knowledge and learn more, you might discover the idea of "soul contracts." This is the theory that two or more individuals choose life scenarios prior to birth. They choose relationships and family ties based on the lessons they wish to learn in the human form.

There is conjecture among some spiritual groups that soul growth can advance more quickly through human incarnations than in spirit form. Therefore, people who are connected through soul agreements choose to hang out together for a variety of different reasons. Imagine a conversation between soul buddies saying, "Wow, it would be really cool if next time around we could arrange to be siblings, business partners, lovers, or whatever…"

Soul contracts are also sometimes based on "tough love." For example, a soul may want to experience rejection, abandonment, or some other difficult emotions in the human life classroom. Consider this when you look back on the experiences in life that were difficult but caused you to grow. How about that well-known phrase: "That which doesn't kill me makes me stronger"? Could the experience itself have been ordered up ahead of time so that your soul could gain that strength?

How about the person you labeled as "evil," that person who put you "through hell"? If another soul has agreed to take on the role of nemesis, then try looking into the eyes of an enemy. You may be surprised to see a friendly-soul looking lovingly back at you.

You might reject this out of hand, or you might return to this theory in ten years and do some more digging. But when you look at the people who died a sudden or violent death, those who took their own lives, the unmotivated deaths and the questions that remain long after the departure of a loved one, take comfort in the fact that there may be a spiritual explanation that is far higher and deeper than our human logic can comprehend. It alters our very understanding of the word "death" and casts a new light on the nature of time.

This perspective of soul contracts doesn't have to be fully accepted for it to create a positive benefit in our lives. Just the most basic knowledge can lead us to consider forgiveness where we might have previously been closed to it.

Equilibrium

My journey is settled now. I have made peace with my past and have discovered equilibrium in my life. I am content to have my gift and to have fully discovered how to use it.

I would be happy to either expand my work into all different areas of communication around the world or to continue on as I am now, steadily helping others find closure. I put my path ahead into the hands of Spirit.

In the same way that I have found closure on my own journey, I hope that this book helps you find closure with your grief, and that you will return to it as a source of reassurance and logic. Moving forward to the next chapter in your life is something to be celebrated. You will look back on your emergence from the grieving experience as that moment you took a great leap forward.

The Leap Forward

Life presents us with great leaps forward from time to time, often in response to admirable efforts on our part. The efforts may have exhausted us to the point where we feel no further progress can be made; then, just as the darkest hour is right before the dawn, a new opening occurs and we are uplifted. Like that emergence from the clouds and fog, you're suddenly there.

In conclusion to this book, I would like to share an experience that was a leap forward for me, and which in turn provided a great many people with an uplifting experience.

I had given a small group sitting for employees of the Pala Resort in San Diego, California. The head of marketing was so excited that she came up with an idea: to have me do an evening event in their huge ballroom for their hotel guests and the local San Diego residents. In order to promote the event, my face was put on giant billboards along the freeways. (Yikes!) It ended up being a sold-out crowd. I was scared to death and excited at the same time.

Until this point, I'd only done sittings for individuals and small groups. I'd never done a demonstration for a large audience. And this was huge—seven hundred people! This became sort of a mediumship milestone for me. The "scared to death" part made itself known to me, but this time I was finally able to say internally, "I see you!" and then put the fear over to one side.

Fear will always be with us; it's up to us as individuals to keep it from getting in our way. I'm very aware of that internal voice that used to try and pull me off course. For so many years, I let it have its way and put aside the exploration of my gift. But eventually I found a way to live with it. It's not that it disappeared—I just embraced it and accepted it as part of me. Remember: fear and doubt are experienced by the general as well as the foot soldier, but the general has learned to deal with his fear; he can acknowledge it, but he will not allow it to rule over him.

I've included my self-doubting internal monologue below for a number of reasons. It lets you know that I'm still just a guy and still normal enough to have normal emotions. I didn't become some spiritual superman who now exists on another plane, oblivious to our day-to-day concerns, and I promise you I'll stay that way!

And more importantly, you can experience the gigantic uplift I received from pushing through to another level of my abilities. Shared experiences are both enlightening and educational, and this might help you with your own perspectives on how human emotions are interwoven with the process of connecting with Spirit.

Pala Casino and Resort, San Diego, California

I was about to go onstage, but first I peeked through the curtain.

Oh, my God, the place is packed! Seven hundred people! I wish they hadn't told me the head count. Why am I so freaked out? They're not here to see me. They're here to "see" them—the spirits. I hope you show up. I'm counting on you. I feel like my legs are going to give out. What if

I walk out in front of the audience and I just fall on the floor? What the hell is wrong with me? I've done this for years—13,000 sittings! But not for seven hundred people at once. Oh, God. Okay. I know how to talk to the dead! I'm really good at it. My stomach. I think I'm going to throw up. What if I get a sudden case of diarrhea or I wet my pants? I'd be a laughingstock! What if I trip on a cord going into the audience and fall flat on my face into some lady's lap? And worse, what if the spirits decide, "Nah. I don't feel like it tonight." And they stay home?

I kept trying to give myself a pep talk, to calm my nerves. It wasn't working yet.

Remember all those years ago when you were just starting out? Remember that first time you saw one of these demonstrations? When you were trying to figure out what to do with this "gift"? James Van Praagh walked out onstage. You had no idea what to expect. Then, remember when you saw the girl in Spirit with the long blond hair running through the room, and James did, too? You knew then that this is what you're supposed to be doing. And here you are. Now, it's your turn.

Okay, Tim, just breathe. See that white light and the golden ball floating down into your crown chakra. You're really good at meditating now! Shoot, did I flush the toilet in the dressing room? Tim, you didn't even use the toilet. Stop being so OCD. You know what you're doing. Remember that. Wait a second! That dream last year! I had a dream that I was here! And there was a huge crowd. I was freaking out at first in the dream; I thought, I'd never do that! But then the dream turned out great. It all went really well. Why don't I believe more in my dreams? I went to India because of one. And that turned out pretty great.

"And with that, ladies and gentlemen, I introduce to you … medium Tim Braun."

Okay. The crowd is applauding. There's no turning back now. It's your turn, Tim.

The energy from the audience (and Spirit) blasted me when I walked onstage. The spirits showed up en masse! They were everywhere. It felt like I was being bombarded. They all started talking at once, trying to take cuts in the spiritual message line. I tried to shush them with my mind, asking them to wait their turn, that I needed to say a few words to the audience! They finally calmed down.

As I faced the audience, I felt exhilarated and terrified all at once. But then, once I really looked at them, I felt this connection, and I became linked to all the people staring at me, hoping for a message. How odd to feel that strong connection, having spent years of my life like such an outcast, so disconnected from everything, including myself. This new feeling was extraordinary. I finally understood that, in this moment, every one of my challenges on this journey had been worth it. Worth the entire struggle, the uncertainty, the emptiness. I took a breath, looked at the audience, and began…

"Hi, everyone. What a crowd! I'm so glad you're all here. As you know, I'm Tim Braun. I'm from Southern California. I grew up in a very Catholic family, the youngest of six kids. My oldest brother unfortunately is a diagnosed paranoid schizophrenic, so we were both hearing voices and having visions at the same time. What a household, right? I am extremely grateful I turned out to be a medium instead of schizophrenic. It took me a long time to come to terms with my gift. And now I celebrate it. So thank you all for coming tonight."

When they all started to applaud, I knew I was going to be okay.

"Thank you! Thank you. Now, let's start with a simple meditation. I like to do that to clear the energy in the room and clear our minds. It's sort of like erasing a chalkboard. Everyone close your eyes. See a golden ball of energy starting at your feet. See it slowly move up your body. Feel its warmth. Feel it healing and relaxing you. Feel it releasing any tension. As it moves through your body, feel the energy. Now imagine it moving through your heart chakra and release any area in your life where you have a lack of love. Feel it moving through your solar plexus and see it changing color to a beautiful emerald green. Let the energy flow through the top of your head. And finally see the energy as raindrops flowing freely. Good. Now open your eyes."

Suddenly I could feel the entire room vibrating.

"I must tell all of you, I'm feeling a lot of energy here tonight. There are many children here in Spirit. But before we get to that, let's open it up to some questions."

Arms shot up all around the room. A woman shouted, "Tim, what happens to you when you're doing this work?"

"That's a good question, and one I get a lot. I see, hear, and sense things—energy. I do this work using all the "clair senses"—clairvoyance, clairaudience, and clairsentience. I see images, hear voices, and sense Spirit. Sometimes they're faint images and voices, sometimes they're outlines. And sometimes Spirit is as clear as you sitting here in front of me. Okay, let's have another question. Yes, you over in the corner."

"What's it like being a medium?"

"A typical day in my life as a medium may involve being 'shot,' 'stabbed,' 'murdered,' having a 'heart attack,' and 'dying of cancer.' I'm actually feeling how they passed. Good thing my partner is a healer! I don't actually get hurt, but I feel what they felt. So it's not just the mental energy that takes a toll, it's the actual physical aspect of feeling their deaths that can wear me out. But don't worry; it also has the opposite effect. Spirit can uplift me, energize me, and make me feel like I'm on the best drugs ever! "Recently the spirit of a man came through in a sitting. It was this woman's husband. He was the happiest guy! I felt like I was floating. He was laughing. He actually got me in hysterics. Turns out he died in a horrible car accident and his body was burned beyond recognition. He came to me in this very disfigured image when he passed and showed me what he looks like now. It was shocking. But he was happy! Go figure. You just never know.

"And by the way, everyone, just because Spirit is on the Other Side doesn't mean they're completely happy or evolved. They have struggles and lessons to learn on that side just like we do over here. They just have a different perspective and experience. They can definitely teach us a lot, and they've taught me so much. But it's important to understand that we teach them, too. It's a give and take. The thing to remember is that we're always connected to them."

And I couldn't believe how connected I felt. I was so relieved I didn't throw up or trip over anyone, or worse.

"Okay, one more question and then we'll get started. Yes, you sir, over there in the green shirt."

"Tim, do you ever get signs when you're not being a medium and you're just out in life doing normal things?"

"Signs? Yes. I had two amazing ones a few hours ago. While I was driving here, this eagle flew right over my windshield. Then right after that, there was this beautiful butterfly that was flying along with me the rest of the way. I took these signs to mean I'm being guided tonight, that I'm not alone, that we're all connected. If I have learned anything with this gift, it's that we're all connected.

"Okay, now I want to ask all of you a question: How many of you have ever been to a medium before? Oh, just three hands? So you're all 'veterans' of this work! Well, this is going to be an adventure for all of us. But I do ask you to keep your expectations in check. Just try to stay open if you can. I also want to point out that, unfortunately, I won't be able to give messages to everyone, but you all will benefit in some way. You may not know how right now, but something may connect with you in the days to come."

I took a breath and focused.

"I'm getting pulled to this side of the room. I'm feeling a strong sensation all over my body. My stomach really hurts. It's in knots. I think some sort of drug is involved. I'm picking up on a young male energy, young like twenty years old. It seems like he died because of a drug overdose. I think this is for you, ma'am. Yes, you in the blue sweater. Yes. What is your name?"

"Kelly."

Kelly sat there in shock and disbelief that maybe the message was for her. I could see and sense so much heaviness and sadness.

"Sorry, I forgot your name already. I'm really bad with names. Oh, yes, that's right. Kelly. Kelly. Kelly. I will remember it now. Does this make sense to you, Kelly?"

The tears started flowing down her cheeks when I asked the question. All she could do was nod. She closed her eyes for a moment. I wondered if she was reliving the experience of losing her son all over again.

"Yes. He was my son. It was heroin."

"Now I understand why I'm feeling so sick all over my body. I've never taken heroin. So, everyone, this is what I meant by feeling the physical sensations of how someone passed. This is so intense. Your son is talking a mile a minute. He's saying, 'Mom, I'm okay. Now he's saying, 'Look at my abs, Mom!' He's pulling up his shirt like this and showing off his abs to me. He's posing like he's at one of those body-building competitions. Do you understand?"

Then Kelly's intense sorrow began to melt away. She smiled as she remembered what she loved about her son. She even started to laugh as she watched me "pose" to imitate what her son was doing on the Other Side. It was as if she was seeing her son again in the flesh.

And then she said: "Yes! I do understand. My son worked out a lot. He was so obsessed with the P90X workout. He loved exercise and fitness. He was always moving his body. It was such a shock that he died the way he did."

"Now he's showing me… Oh, this is interesting. Was there a fire alarm that went off the other day in your house, Kathy?"

"It's *Kelly*. My name's Kelly."

"I'm so sorry, Kelly. I should write the names down in my palm. But I do have to say, my forgetfulness can be a blessing. I've found that when I keep repeating the name of the sitter over and over again, it helps to connect them with their loved one on the Other Side. Kelly, did the fire alarm go off in your house?"

"Yes! And it scared me. I thought the house was going to burn down or something. I ran around to all the rooms looking for flames. But there was nothing. Not even a candle burning. I couldn't figure it out."

"Well, your son is saying he did that. And now he's laughing. Like he's sort of proud. Also, I have to tell you, I'm getting that this was not murder or a suicide, if you were wondering about that. I hope this helps."

Kelly looked so relieved. She didn't share if she had been worried that her son was murdered or took his own life, but I could tell she was happy to get the information. She was smiling; her eyes were so much brighter now.

"Yes, it helps. Thank you, Tim."

"Thank you, Kelly."

This was such a powerful message that lasted just a few minutes. It was like I was this catalyst, able to take Kelly on her son's journey as he overdosed from the heroin and then when he crossed over. I was so happy to deliver the message that her son was happy and still around her. And it was wonderful to see Kelly's transformation from being so distraught over her son's traumatic death to gaining such a sense of peace when she realized her son was okay. This is why this work is so rewarding for me.

"I'll take a few more questions. Yes. You, sir. What's your question?"

"Tim, you said you grew up in a Catholic family. Do they support you doing this work?"

"No, they don't. But, they're praying for all of us right now—especially me!

"Okay. Over here, in the middle of the room. There's an energy I'm getting here. I think it's for you. No, sorry. That row. I'm having a hard time pinpointing this. You know, sometimes Spirit gets a little mixed up, too. They can send me on a wild goose chase trying to decipher their messages and who they're for. I guess they're busy assessing their life on the Other Side. They can get distracted, too!

Okay. Yes. Yes. I hear you. In case you're wondering what I'm doing right now, having a conversation with myself—well, not exactly. I'm listening to Spirit's instructions. They're trying to tell me whom they want to connect with. Sometimes it's like listening to Russian. A lot of this work is about listening. That's why I always tell sitters who want to get signs and messages from their loved ones on their own to pay attention and be present in their daily lives. Sorry, everyone, I can get as distracted as Spirit does sometimes."

Spirit was yanking me in all directions at this point. They were all talking at once again. Then the one spirit came through loud and clear. It was really intense. I knew she was someone's child. It was another tragic death. Although I've been the middleman for so many messages from children trying to connect with a parent, it's always so difficult for that parent who has lost their child. But I kept going. I knew this message had to get delivered.

"No, not you, sir. This is for the woman in yellow. Yes. Wow. I'm feeling this strong sensation in my body. It's a jolt. My whole body aches. I'm getting that someone, a female, was ejected from a motorcycle. Does that make sense to you, ma'am? What is your name?"

The woman in yellow put her hand over her mouth, stunned. I felt her intense anxiety. She said almost in a whisper, "I'm Shirley. And yes, she's my daughter…"

Shirley could hardly speak. It was like each word was so painful to utter. Then she started to cry. It's so difficult to keep myself from falling apart emotionally when recounting these tragic deaths. I could feel her deep anguish.

"She was thrown from a motorcycle."

"Oh. I'm so sorry. Your daughter is coming through very clearly. She's talking about her brother. She's very agitated. Is he still here with us? He is? Okay. Well, your daughter is saying he shouldn't feel bad about what happened. Is this making sense to you?"

Then Shirley's eyes widened. She was surprised, and yet this made tremendous sense to her. I could feel more intense sadness coming from her. It was like she was in a double whammy of emotional pain. She started to cry again.

"Yes. Yes. It is making sense. Her brother, my son, keeps saying he wants to join her on the Other Side. He says he can't bear life without her now."

"Your daughter is saying over and over that he shouldn't feel responsible. She wants him to know that and that she's fine. Does she also have four cats that have passed? I see four cats over there with her."

Shirley started to smile. "Yes! All my daughter's cats died before she did."

"Okay. Well, now she's talking about that picture of her in the paper. Did you put her picture with her obituary?"

"Yes. I did put her picture in the paper."

"Well, I'm sorry to tell you this, Shirley, but your daughter is saying that she really doesn't like the picture. She's very insistent. She keeps saying, 'Tell my mom I don't like that picture of me. I don't like it. I don't like it.'

"It's always so interesting, everybody, about what comes through when I'm doing this work. Spirit has their own agenda. I have no idea why they focus on certain things. Sometimes, they just want to validate that it's them. They'll bring up the most trivial thing just so the sitter will recognize who they are."

As I was doing my own demonstration onstage, I kept thinking about everything that led me up to this moment. I remembered all those years ago sitting in the audience at James Van Praagh's demonstration, in awe of him being able to do this on the spot. Just the thought of being up there terrified me. Not to mention many disastrous attempts to meditate (luckily I got better at that). And now I could hardly believe I was standing on this stage delivering messages from the Other Side. I was still petrified walking onstage that night, but now, in the middle of the demonstration, I felt so at home. This was where I belonged.

As I strolled around the room talking to the audience, Spirit led me to a woman sitting toward the back. The closer I got to her, the more intense the pain was.

"I'm feeling a sharp pain in the back of my head right now, on the left side. Right about here. It feels like a gunshot. I think this is for you, yes, you in the dark blue dress, sitting on the aisle. I'm getting a male figure… He was murdered. He was shot in the back of the head."

This was such a powerful moment. It's always so difficult to connect with a murder victim and to see the loved ones in such pain.

"Was he your husband, ma'am?"

"Yes. My husband was shot and killed…" The woman struggled to share the information. Then she burst into tears. "You're right. He was murdered."

Then in the midst of this darkness, I felt a light energy. Almost blissful. The man was laughing. I couldn't figure it out. But it's not my job to judge the information, just to deliver it.

"Well, I have to tell you. It's strange, he just keeps laughing. He's saying, 'If my wife can hear my laughter she'll know it's me.' Does that make sense to you?"

The woman's face suddenly lit up! She had the biggest smile. She even started *to giggle*. "Oh my God, yes! My husband always laughed a lot."

"Now your husband is showing me a burger place. Johnny's Burgers? Do you understand?"

The woman was so energized and excited now. The transformation was palpable. And the intense pain I felt in the back of my head was gone.

"Yes! Yes! Absolutely! Johnny's was our favorite place to eat."

When I get these specific details from Spirit, it's incredibly exhilarating. It's like receiving some sort of award, my gift is validated.

I delivered one more message for the woman whose husband was murdered.

"There's one last thing. Your husband is talking about a cruise. Were you both planning to go on a cruise?"

"Yes. We had plans to go on one right before he died. "

"He's telling me he really wants you to take that cruise... for both of you. He wants you to promise to do that."

I could see the sadness come back to her, but it was different now. It was mixed with peacefulness.

"I promise. I will do that. Thank you, Tim."

"I can't believe how the evening has flown by. We've got just a few minutes left. I'll take two more questions from the audience. Yes?"

"What's it like over there, on the Other Side. Do they tell you?"

"Another great question. And one I get asked a lot. It's very individualistic from sitter to sitter. Some in Spirit say they greet children as they pass. Others have jobs, the same house they lived in. They're focused on making the connection with their loved one. I can tell you that just because a person crosses over, it doesn't elevate them to star Spirit status. There is a lot of work to do over there, just like over here. But what I do know is, it's very different. They're not bogged down with a body. They can zip around more quickly and communicate with thought. It seems like it's pretty wonderful there. Okay. One final question. Yes, you in the white."

"Tim, what have you learned from all the messages you've delivered? From the spirits? Do they have the secret to happiness or something?"

"Unfortunately, as far as I know, they don't have the secret to happiness. Or they're just not telling me. What I have learned is, we've all got our own journey to travel. Seems pretty obvious. It's all about having as many experiences as we can and learning from those experiences. But I'm afraid that when we get over there, we still have to work on ourselves.

"They tell me it takes hundreds of years to go from 'freshman to sophomore to junior to senior' in the 'college' across the veil, and that's why we incarnate here to Earth, to speed up the process of evolving when we go back to Spirit side. The more we can get out of our own way by living life to the fullest, without regrets, and learn to love completely and unconditionally, the faster we'll progress over there. Thank you all for this powerful evening."

As I walked offstage, I realized, more than ever, what my purpose is in doing this work. It's pretty straightforward. As I've always said: I am the middleman, here to deliver messages. And if a handful of people walked out of there tonight feeling a little more connected to the person they missed so much, if they felt more at peace, and then to have the entire audience experience and witness the messages from the Other Side with them, then I think I have done my job.

11

Finding Closure: Insights from a Lifetime of Mediumship

The first time I recall having a sense of the work I was meant to do was after I read a book about two hospice nurses who heard countless stories of their patients seeing the Other Side before they died. They all were seeing different family and friends and greeting them. As they wrote about "walking their patients to the edge" to cross over, something clicked inside of me. I knew I was meant to do this work.

In a recent interview, I was asked, "How has being a medium impacted your own life?" The answer is as simple and straightforward as I am: talking to the dead has taught me how to live.

I've learned how to be open, how to listen, how to pay attention, and how to be present, simply because I have to do all those things in order to do my job. Being the middleman, the message bearer, and a connector to Spirit has taught me how to be a better human being.

I've seen, heard, sensed, and experienced all kinds of transitions, from tragic deaths to peaceful ones. I've sat across from countless mothers, fathers, sisters, brothers, daughters, sons, friends, and other family members and witnessed their intense grief and emotional devastation from the loss of a loved one.

Then, many times, I have been lucky enough to witness their transformation from the emotional pain they bear to finding some peace of mind when they get a message from that loved one on the Other Side. I've seen their tears morph into smiles. That is why I do what I do. I'm always grateful for my gift, and especially that I was able come to terms with it and allowed this ability back into my life.

The Energy

I love what I do—helping others heal their grief by connecting them with their loved ones. But it does overwhelm me at times. When I'm not doing this work, I get anxious. When I am doing this work, all the energy that is pent up in me is flowing.

Now that I'm more experienced, I've found it's easier to just accept the challenges of the work rather than to turn the "Spirit spigot" off. When I'm not doing sittings and I want a break, I consciously stop channeling the energy that is coming through. But when I take a few days off, by the third day I start to get anxious. It's not that I'm a workaholic; I just need to keep channeling this energy and bringing it through in order to maintain a balance within myself.

My calling is mediumship. I think maybe because I felt so disconnected growing up, I was hungry to connect in every way possible as an adult.

I'm *not* a therapist or a psychologist. They of course have a different and equally important place in the grieving process.

Empathy

We all can provide a form of support while loved ones deal with the idea of life not being the same after their loss. It's a huge void. They have to learn how to live with the emptiness. I sit with them in their emptiness during the sitting.

Empathy is a big part of this work. When people are dealing with loss, there is a constant search to make sense of their new reality. Everyone grieves differently, but it's important to deal with our feelings, to feel the sadness, and hopefully again find peace and bliss in our lives. It's rewarding to be a part of this process.

The result often offers a sense of closure for the sitter, and sometimes it can also act as an opening to a new relationship with the person who's no longer here physically.

When a sitter comes in with such a heavy, sad energy and I'm able to help transform that in some way, it's the greatest feeling. This is their gift and Spirit's gift to *me*. And I'm forever grateful. I always say, "I work for Spirit. They're my true employers!" If I can provide an hour or even a moment of peace, then I feel like I've done my job.

As I said in the Introduction, my purpose in writing this book is to lift the vibration of the planet through sharing my experiences—not only of becoming a medium but what the journey was like, how much I learned along the way, and how each step in our lives is important, no matter where you're going. I wouldn't trade one step, as difficult as some of them were. All of them taught me a valuable life lesson.

But remember, you don't have to be a medium to raise the vibration of the planet. It's not what you do; it's how you do it. It does not matter what a person's job is; what matters is you do it 110 percent as best as you can.

People tend to exalt those of us who are able to communicate with the Other Side. I don't have the secret to a happy and successful life, except that I know (as Spirit keeps reminding me) that the key lies in the very ingredient we need to connect with them: *love*.

We all know this. It's just such an obvious answer—right in front of our noses, hiding in plain sight. Loving others and ourselves, whether they're here or "over there" … it's no big secret.

But sometimes, maybe because it's so obvious, we just forget. All the questions you have about life, from what I understand, are right here, within us.

With that said, I have received some insights from Spirit regarding certain aspects of life on this side of the veil.

Dying

There is nothing to be afraid of. I know that there is more to this life on Earth, and we're here to be full-time students from the moment we're born until the moment we die. If we have had a lifetime of powerful learning experiences, then we've done what we're meant to be doing as human beings. I always gravitate toward learning new things, being constantly curious and open.

So I concentrate not on dying but on living. That's what I've learned from those who've crossed over. They've taught me the most about living. Death does not discriminate—it evens the playing field no matter who we are, what we do, and how we live. We will all experience it, both with loved ones and ourselves.

Happiness

Ironically this whole process with all the sadness and loss has taught me a lot about happiness. Remember: happiness can emerge even in our darkest hours if we just open our hearts. And I know that for the most part, Spirit is pretty happy on the Other Side.

So don't worry about them! (Remember the decapitated guy?) Spirit has taught me that attaining happiness is very simple. It starts with love.

Fear

If you dwell on fear, you're not able receive; it is a poison that prevents us from living and connecting with those on the Other Side. Fear is a magnet for bad things. An explanation for this: Spirit has told me that thoughts are powerful and that they create our reality. That's where fear begins—with a thought.

Fear can keep us from accepting our gifts and from accepting who we really are. Once we accept ourselves, doors begin to open, showing us the way. It is very difficult to eliminate fear altogether, but it is possible. Fear can be healthy. If you can face it, you can get past it. Fear teaches us to live in the moment.

Regrets

One of the most powerful pieces of advice I've gotten from Spirit is to live without regret. Not so easy, I know. But regret, like guilt, is a waste. It's a sign that you aren't (and haven't) lived fully.

In a sitting with Ed Cook, a friend of his came through who was very well-to-do. He had this gorgeous Corvette that he adored. But he always kept it in the garage, so it wouldn't get a scratch or a dent and so it wouldn't get stolen. He was so afraid that he would lose his precious car. And guess what? He *never* drove it! One of his regrets he shared was not driving his beloved car. He never got to experience what it was meant to do.

So the Corvette story is a metaphor for life. Always take your "Corvette" out for a drive. Don't play it safe and leave it in the garage. You'll miss out on the wonderful experience of driving down the highway with the wind blowing in your hair or face.

One of my own regrets in this life is that I didn't kiss Mother Teresa's feet when I was in India. I was encouraged by everyone there to do it. It was a huge privilege. But my own closed mind, because of my upbringing, prevented me from doing that. I always thought for some reason it wasn't culturally acceptable.

But I really wanted to step out of my comfort zone and kiss her feet. I missed out on this unique opportunity and what would have been such a meaningful experience.

There are all kinds of regrets that I've heard from Spirit over the years, but the regret I've heard most is, "I wished I had said 'I love you' so much more—or even once." So many spirits say they wish they had broken out of their skin, out of their comfort zone, while they were here.

Forgiveness

One of the most powerful things we can do is to forgive. First we must forgive ourselves, then we need to forgive others. I learned this in my own life, growing up feeling so disconnected from my family. I now understand how important forgiveness is. During countless sittings, I've seen forgiveness happen from both sides of the veil. That's where the healing begins.

So much of the grief I've witnessed from Spirit and sitters alike seems to be held in all the missed opportunities of things not said to a loved one when they were alive. Being able to clear the air with them cleans the slate and frees both Spirit and the person left behind.

Prayer

What is the most effective and most powerful prayer? It's pretty simple and doesn't require memorization. Just say "Thank you." Some of us feel disconnected from our religion, don't have a spiritual path, or just don't know how to pray. The best thing to do, when we wake up every morning and go to sleep every night, is to just start saying thank you. This is a good place to start.

Organized Religion

Whether you're Catholic, Methodist, Episcopalian, Jewish, Muslim, or a member of any other religion, chances are the doctrine doesn't usually enthusiastically condone going to mediums and seeking out messages from the dead. Organized religion is like a coat we wear on this side. "When we cross over, the coats come off," says fellow medium Robert Brown.

When we review our lives, what matters is not what religion we practiced but how we lived our lives. Did we practice that religion with integrity? And most importantly, did we love unconditionally?

Love has the power to connect. That's what Spirit says is needed in order to get messages from the Other Side.

Living

If we live each day awake, alive, being grateful and saying yes to new experiences, we won't have regrets and we can learn to be happy in the moment.

If we love fully, we'll have love in return, no matter what religion we are or what spiritual path we're on. If we don't let fear trample us and allow for mistakes, we will foster forgiveness (of ourselves and others). The question is, did you learn from those mistakes? If you truly learned something, then you are living life to the fullest and you're doing what you came here to do.

Someone once said, "It's not what happens to us that matters; it's how we deal with what happens." And if we open up our minds and hearts to what we can't necessarily see and trust that dying is a transition—a beginning and not the end—we may be able to connect with that person we long for who is now on the Other Side. We might even gain a new connection, a new relationship with them that we didn't have on this side.

What I've learned on this journey is to accept ourselves for who we really are.

Follow the path that we're called to travel on. Let it lead us and guide us, no matter how rocky, uncertain, and frightening it may be at times. Just keep going. Trust that you'll find your way. The most important thing is to give 110 percent of ourselves and do the best we can with integrity. When you die and go to the Other Side, you'll review your life based on how you lived it, not on what you did.

Do whatever you do in life as if you were given a gift. We all have gifts and can help to make life on the earth plane a little easier if these gifts are shared. I have gotten to a place in life where I can sit on a trail overlooking the ocean with my two dogs and say to myself, "I am making a little difference in sharing this gift."

It's funny, I'm only a forty-five-minute drive from my parents' house in Whittier, but to me it seems like worlds away—a lifetime away. I think back to being that six-year-old kid who heard and saw Spirit for the first time, so afraid of what it meant and pushing it away.

Today, I'm using that gift in ways I never imagined. Now I look forward each day to opening the door to the Other Side, ready to receive the messages. And I'm ready for my next chapter.

12

The Sitter's Guide

The sitting. It's more than just sitting in a chair across from the medium, waiting (and hoping) that your loved one will have a message for you. As I have said in previous chapters, I have no control over who comes through and what messages they have to share.

What I can do as a medium is create the space for connecting and raise my energetic vibration as Spirit lowers theirs. As the sitter, there are many things you can do to prepare yourself for a wonderful and memorable experience. Remember: they want to connect with you as much as you want to connect with them.

What follows are some sitter guidelines.

Preparing for the Sitting

Thoughts Create Reality

Thoughts are things. What you think about manifests into life experiences. The same is true when you're trying to connect with your loved one. It's important to see them, feel them, remember them on this side, and love them.

Create Loving Energy

It's simple, and something you can start doing hours, days, even weeks before your session. Think of your loved one and feel love for them. Really feel it. Don't just think loving thoughts—feel the love in your entire body. This will raise the energetic vibration. Spirit responds most to love. Help them connect with you.

Invite Your Loved One to the Sitting

This is powerful and important, just like feeling the love you have for them. Talk to them on the way (and hours, days, and weeks before), in your mind or out loud (probably in private and not as you walk down the street, unless you want to pretend you're on your cell phone), and ask them to come to the sitting.

This puts out positive energy for you and them. Try not to get into a desperate or demanding space. That keeps your loved one from connecting. Keep the energy light and inviting.

Meditate

As we discussed earlier, this is the most powerful way to connect to yourself, which in turn helps you to connect with your loved one in Spirit. By meditating, you can clear your mind, which opens the channels of communication. If your mind is filled with negative, random thoughts (the "monkey mind"), it can act as a roadblock, preventing those precious messages from coming through and reaching you.

There are meditations in Chapter 6 that work well for preparing for the sitting, as well as helping to connect after the sitting.

Bring Special Mementos

Whether it's a picture, a piece of jewelry, a watch, or any object that was special to that person, bring it to the sitting. Hold it in your hand or wear it, and think of them.

Again, feel the love you have for them. It can act as a powerful energetic connector and a magnet to bring their presence to you.

During the Sitting

Be Present

The most important thing to bring to the sitting is your presence—

not only being there physically, but being there mentally and emotionally, moment by moment.

Leave all worries, concerns, and thoughts about the past and the future at the door. Remember the pro tennis player leaving his worries on a spot outside the court. If you've done your preparation, you most likely will already be in the moment and ready to focus. This is your time with your loved one who is in Spirit, so it's important to treat it as a very precious experience, savoring every moment.

Breathe

At the beginning of my sittings, both the sitter and I do a brief meditation involving deep breathing. We take three deep breaths and clear our minds.

Again, if you've been meditating in the hours, days, or even weeks prior to the sitting, you'll be able to clear your mind in the session with ease.

Listen

This is critical. Although most sittings are recorded (mine always are), you still want to pay attention to everything I'm saying. There is nothing like the live experience when you first receive the message.

And it's important when a message or specific detail is conveyed that you're paying attention so that you can recognize that it's your loved one. This helps the sitting go smoothly and helps with the connection.

Speak Sparingly

The less information you give the medium, the better. I always ask for first names only when the sitter makes the appointment, and I ask that you not volunteer a lot of information in the sitting. It's important to keep the channels of communication clear for Spirit to come through. If you are constantly offering details, it will muddy the sitting.

Respond with a Yes or No

This is ideal. A medium may ask, "Does this make sense to you?" or "Do you understand?"

We need some confirmation that this is indeed your loved one. In previous chapters, I describe sitter stories where Spirit will share a funny or odd detail to show that it's them. It's important for the sitter to be listening intently.

Of course, when you start getting messages, you'll most likely be energized and want to start talking to your loved one. But if you can stay in the receiving mode, it will help to get clear and stronger messages. When you're present—listening more than speaking—this will create a more successful sitting experience.

Manage Expectations

You can't control if your loved one will come through and, when they do, what message they will share, but you can control your own perception of the experience, and that includes expectations.

It's completely understandable that you are very anxious to connect. The sitting can be a powerful emotional roller coaster, but it's important to understand that there can be many reasons for that particular person not showing up or not in the way you expect.

Also, be prepared for others you did not expect to come through. They may surprise you with important and poignant messages!

Keep an Open Mind

Just like managing expectations, it's important to be open. Mediums will have sitters who are skeptical. (I was skeptical of my own gift for a long time!) It's healthy to have a little skepticism, but if you come in with an "arms closed" attitude, you will block the messages.

Keeping an open mind simply helps energetically. An open mind in other parts of life can open us up to wonderful experiences. Why not with a sitting? There are many things that we can't explain that require us to have faith.

Connect After the Sitting

When your session is done, you don't have to be. Keep the connection going by using all the "Preparing for the Sitting" techniques and the suggestions in the "Raising Your Vibration" chapter. You may start feeling a stronger presence after this experience. Help your loved one to keep connecting with you.

Remember, you can create a new relationship with them, which can help you heal the grief and the emptiness. This can be a positive, uplifting new chapter for you.

13

Frequently Asked Questions

Because mediumship and the afterlife are so mysterious, I am exposed to a constant state of curiosity from both my sitters and the people I come across in everyday life.

By now, you know my journey and how I became a medium. But there are still questions. So many people wonder what's beyond this life as we know it, and how are some people able to get a glimpse? I do have to point out, though, that just because I'm a medium doesn't necessarily mean I have the answers to the meaning of life.

I'm just like you—a human being trying to understand what this life experience is all about. I just happen to have a gift of connecting with the dead. They don't have all the answers, either. But I can say, I have learned a lot along the way from all the sittings, and all the spirits who've come through. Here are some of the questions I'm asked the most.

What has been your most memorable sitting to date?
This sitting opens the book. It was the mother and wife of a man who died in the Twin Towers on 9/11. I had no idea what was happening as I was feeling the jolt of the plane plowing into the building and then the inferno. My whole body was in pain. It was very intense but well worth it to bring some peace to the family.

Which stage of grief is the sitter usually in when they come to you?
It varies. They are most often in the early stages of grief. That's why they come to me. They are in such pain and want badly to connect

with their loved ones. They want to know they're okay. And what's interesting is when I do connect, Spirit is just as anxious to know their family is okay on this side.

I always recommend that sitters wait approximately three months before they come to me, but it varies from sitter to sitter, depending on the loss they've experienced. A person who dies from cancer is different from someone who took their own life. The state of the sitter's readiness depends on that and how ready they are to connect. But often their loved one needs time to transition.

What is the biggest barrier for a sitter, or anyone who has lost someone, to connect with that person who has passed on?
Mainly skepticism. When they come in with their arms crossed tightly, it's a barrier to connecting. If they have a "prove it to me" attitude, the sitting will be difficult and I will have a hard time bringing in the love one who's crossed over.

Also, having expectations, which can make the sitter impatient and nervous. These things can be huge barriers. The best thing is to come in with love and an open mind. Spirit needs us to help them connect. It takes a lot of energy to communicate from across the veil.

Why are some sittings more powerful than others? What makes Spirit come through so strongly?
Some sittings have been amazingly accurate, but the sitter will say it was "very interesting." It's frustrating because I felt it was amazing because of all the evidence.

In other sittings I will feel like the connection could have been stronger, yet the sitter will say, "You are amazing". Each sitting is a unique experience for both the sitter and me.

Just like the previous question, if you can remove all barriers within yourself before you come into the sitting and during the sitting, you most likely will have a powerful experience. Having a receptive, open mind is a magnet for connecting with your loved one.

Why do spirits stay around near the earth plane? Why are some anchored here? Is it because of unresolved issues or work here? Do some not stick around?

The dead can still be attached to the love of the family. Yes, sometimes there are unresolved issues that they want to convey in a sitting. They need closure, too. Or maybe they want to continue living their life like an earthbound being and just want to stay close to their loved ones.

It's not always true that they feel they're in a better place. Sometimes the dead are not happy or content about having crossed over. Often it just takes time for them to adjust to their new reality. But I have to say, most of the time, they are elated to be on the Other Side.

What's it like on the Other Side? Do spirits ever describe it to you in detail?

Spirit says how bright and bold the colors are. They talk a lot about how freeing it is not to have a body. But it's very individual for every spirit. And just because Spirit has crossed over it doesn't mean the slate is wiped clean of struggles. They're still learning. In fact, their learning is at an accelerated pace. We take over to the Other Side our fears, insecurities, and other negative traits.

I have actually heard the music and seen the flowers. The music is so powerful. It's hard to describe. It's more than listening; it's an entire experience. The flowers are vibrant. And I've seen colors that I've never seen before.

I feel that when my time comes it will be something I look forward to. It puts everything in perspective. For me, I can be on either side. But for now, I am human.

Are there bad spirits that have come through? How do you handle them?

They do exist. I am aware of them and know it's important not to allow that energy in. It's the job of a medium to keep their energy pure and positive to keep away any dark energy.

That is why I begin and end each sitting with a protective guided meditation. My meditation is to clear the bad spirits.

One time I had a bad feeling about a spirit. My sitter's uncle had molested her and he wanted to come through to make amends. He was in a lower vibration.

The sitter absolutely did not want to connect with him, even if he wanted to make things right. I honored her wish. Frankly, I was glad she made that choice. I had a very bad feeling about him, and I didn't want to bring in that dark energy.

What is that dark energy like? Think of a beautiful brilliant day—blue skies, soft winds. Then go to the polar opposite—a dark, gloomy day filled with a heavy, sad energy. That's the best way to describe this.

Have you ever gone to a spiritualist church? What was your experience?

Yes, in the United Kingdom. They have a lot of the spiritualist churches there. They're very interesting. We don't have many here. The entire service is like one long sitting. The medium or mediums do readings on whomever they connect with in the audience. It's very similar to the demonstrations we do here. They do those there as well, but mostly in these spiritualist church settings. I learned a lot from them. They are definitely something to experience.

What's the wildest thing that has happened to you as a medium away from the "office," when you're on your day off—say, in line

at the grocery store or something?

It was around 11 pm. I had gotten up to go to the bathroom. When I turned on the light in the bathroom, there was a woman—a spirit—hanging from the ceiling. It was scary, of course.

Yeah, even we mediums can be sickened by bizarre happenings. When she came through at my first sitting the next day, I understood. She was a little impatient. See? Spirit can have a few human foibles! It all worked out fine. Her husband was grateful she came through and that he received so much healing.

What is your opinion on suicide?

There are so many reasons for suicide and circumstances around this. I agree with the Native Americans' belief that those who take their lives are taking themselves home and we should honor their choice. I know mediums and spiritual leaders will often say it's a selfish act, but I don't want to make that call.

What is your opinion on reincarnation?

Well, I don't believe we come back as ants, polar bears, or a gardenia plant. But I do strongly believe in Soul Groups. So in terms of reincarnation, I believe it happens within our Soul Groups. As a human, we reincarnate within our particular soul group to work out any past karma.

What is your opinion of angels and guides? Do we all have them?

I do think angels and guides are among us. They are not our loved ones who have crossed over. It's like they're a different "spirit species," if you will. They have never been human. They are more evolved and are on a different plane, and that's why they can guide us in our human experience. They've always been angels and guides.

Frankly, I think angels and guides are one and the same. It's a fascinating topic. I don't connect with them in sittings. My connections come from the human beings who've crossed over—although I do have my own angels and guides who help me, otherwise I would not be able to do this work on my own.

What about pets who've crossed over?
Pets are always interesting. It's fascinating to hear them speak. They don't actually have voices, more like "messages of all-knowing" that I get. But pets can come through very strongly.

Recently, in one of my demonstrations, this woman who had been killed in a motorcycle accident had several cats that had died before she did. And there she was, on the Other Side, surrounded by her precious felines. She was so happy to be reunited with them, and they were thrilled to have their owner back.

Do you connect with babies who have crossed over?
Yes. Often their deaths are due to miscarriages, stillbirths, and abortions. Both babies and pets are the highest vibration of love. They don't care about a person's ethnicity, creed, or sexual orientation. All they want to do is give unconditional love.

Do spirits evolve when they cross over? Or do some get stuck?
Most spirits do evolve. That's the whole point. But each spirit evolves at a different pace. Some are on the fast track, while others take a lot of time. Again, if they were slow to evolve on this side, chances are the same thing will happen on the Other Side.

Do you study mediumship? Do research? Anything to expand your skills now? What's interesting to you in this world? What calls you?

I'm so busy these days that it's hard to do any studying. But I have to say, I'm always learning from my sitters and from Spirit. They're my best teachers! So I'm sort of a perennial "medium student."

I stay open and curious, which helps me to get better at what I do. Occasionally, I will attend a lecture or get together with a medium or a spiritual leader and sort of exchange ideas and experiences.

Do you imagine yourself on the Other Side? What do you see?
Yes! All the time. I hear amazing music and see the most vibrant colors. It's hard to describe. I think it's something that we have to wait and experience when we get there. Maybe that's why there are so few details of the Other Side. But I'm very excited to make my transition—but not just yet, of course! I've got too much to do here! Besides, I love what I'm doing and the life I've created, so I'm not ready to go yet.

Have you ever had a loved one come through?
Surprisingly, I have not connected with my father, friends, or grandparents on the Other Side. I would love to, but I accept that maybe it's not meant to be. Maybe it's similar to psychics trying to do readings on themselves. They usually don't. They're too close to it. I think the same goes for mediums. Or for me, anyway.

Any favorite words or quotes to live by?
Live life to the fullest. Be in the moment. And tell the truth. I've learned that not just from being a medium but from this incredible journey I've had getting to where I am today. It's so important that we live our lives as *we* want to live them and not for what others want us to be. A nurse recently published a study of the top ten regrets of patients on their deathbeds, and the number one regret was, "I wish I'd had the courage to live a life true to

myself, not the life others expected of me." So again, live your life to the absolute fullest.

Once you do that, your world opens up. Mine certainly did.

And I hope that with this book others can be inspired to be who they really are and find their purpose, and have fun in the process!

Oh, I just thought of some words of wisdom that I love: "Life is not about the destination. It's about the journey. So savor each step you take along the way."

Seven Affirmations
for Finding Closure

Speak and repeat these affirmations daily out loud as often as needed, and you will uplift your energy. By repeating them many times, you will incorporate them into your subconscious.

Today, I witness everything with love.

Today, I forgive myself for everything.

Today, I trust my inner wisdom.
Today, I am open to all possibilities before me and know that only good can result from my changing.

Today, I am free of all problems, all fear, and all possibilities of failure.

Today, I express a unique expression of divine love.
Today, I align with love in each person.

Acknowledgments

M y heartfelt thanks to the large, growing number of people who grace my life; you have made me what I am today. Your friendship, love, and affection continue to uplift and humble me. Just as so many people have helped me on my journey, so many have helped with this book. It takes a lot of support and encouragement, and for that I am deeply grateful.

My clients, past and present: your commitment to healing and finding closure is always so powerful for me, and helping you is so rewarding or me. You have all touched me.

Bill Moller, Donna Moller, Ruthie Frazee, James Van Praagh, Robert Brown, Donna Repp, Lynn Mitchell and Steve Stein, Sammy Gahn, Stacy Justis, Mary Helen Hensley, Asha Blake, Keith Cohen, Laurie St. Clare, Ute Ville, Amanda Mehalick and Brandon Camacho at Awakenings Spiritual Bookstore.

Thank you, Findhorn Press. Special thanks to Gail Torr, Thierry Bogliolo, Sabine Weeke, Nicky Leach, and Carol Shaw for your support!

Thank you, Gary Quinn and Anita Gregory for your support and guidance.

Thank you, Tracy Pattin, for your amazing talent and insight!

Thank you, Charlie Watson and Michelle Dotter, for your expertise and efforts.

Thank you, David Swift, for your confidence and support at Pala Casino.

Thank you, Sabine Giger at Giger Verlag Gmbh, Switzerland, Germany, and Austria.

Thank you, Penelope Clark and Jackie Collins for hard work.

Thank you Eli Frankel, Ryan Holcomb and Lauren Counter at Lionsgate-Rogue Atlas.

Thank you, Kevin Stachel, for your friendship, love, trust and patience.

Thank you, Pascal Voggenhubber, for our new friendship.

Thank you, Efis Editore srl Publishing Italy, Loretta Zanuccoli, Elena Benvenuti, Laura Cigolini Gulesu, Antonio Ruccia, Daniele Ruccia, and Davide Cortesi.

Thank you, Arielle Ford, for your insight and guidance.

Thank you, Rev. Sandra Dixon, for your support and hard work.

Special thanks to Rolonda Watts, Marilu Henner, and Rachel Anderson and Emmanuel Itier.

I thank all the thousands of sitters who have come to me to connect with their loved ones over the years. And I thank the thousands of spirits willing to come through, who have delivered messages of hope, love, and inspiration to the ones you've left behind. You are my "employers."

I am forever grateful to all the individuals whose stories are in this book. Ed Cook, Tony and Carol DiRaimondo, Maria Pe, Don Ruetz, Mark D. Stuart, Tracy Pattin, and Peggy Higuchi.

Thank you all for the contributions everyone has made, and anyone who I may have omitted. Thank you! Most of all I am grateful for the opportunity to write this book and for bringing the message all together in this project of love.

Resources and Recommended Reading

Books

Brinkley, Dannion, *Saved by the Light*. HarperOne, 1994/2008.

Brown, Robert. *We Are Eternal*. Warner Books, 2003.

Callanan, Maggie, and Kelley, Patricia. *Final Gifts: Understanding the Special Awareness, Needs, and Communications of the Dying*. Bantam, 1997.

Hurst, Brian Edward, Heaven Can Help, Self-published, 2007

Kübler-Ross MD, Elisabeth. *On Death and Dying*. Scribner, 1997.

Moller, Bill. *The Gift of Hands That Heal*. She-I Publishing, 1998.

Newton, Michael. *Case Studies of Life Between Lives*. Llewellyn publications, 1994.

Newton, Michael. *Destiny of Souls: New Case Studies of Life Between Lives*. Llewellyn, 2000.

Newton, Michael. *Journey of Souls*. Llewellyn Publications, 1994.

Newton, Michael. *Life Between Lives: Hypnotherapy for Spiritual Regression*. Llewellyn Publications, 2004.

Pe, Maria. *Journey To The Upper Realm*. Self-published, 2013.

Quinn, Gary. *The Yes Frequency.* Findhorn Press, 2013

Rogers, Sandi. *Lessons from the Light: In-Sights from a Journey to the Other Side*. Warner Books, Inc., 1995.

Ruetz, Don. *Remember Me*. Self-published, 2014.

Schiff Sarnoff, Harriet. *The Bereaved Parent*. Penguin Books, 1977.

Robert,Schwartz. *Your Soul's Gift*. Whispering Winds Press, 2012

Stuart, Mark D. *Grief Transformed*. Paige Press, 2010.

Van Praagh, James. *Talking To Heaven*. Penguin Group, 1997.

Spiritual Centers

A.R.E. Association for Research and Enlightenment

Edgar Cayce's Association for Research and Enlightenment, Inc. (A.R.E.) is a not-for-profit organization founded in 1931 by Edgar Cayce (1877-1945) to research and explore transpersonal subjects such as holistic health, ancient mysteries, personal spirituality, dreams and dream interpretation, intuition, and philosophy and reincarnation.

www.edgarcayce.org

Lily Dale Assembly

Spiritualist community on Cassadaga Lake that offers daily lectures on the wonders of psychic phenomena, clairvoyant demonstrations, and spiritual healing.

www.lilydaleassembly.com

The Journey Within – Spiritualists' National Church

The Reverend Janet Nohavec founded this church in 1996, and it is the first church in the U.S. to be affiliated with the Spiritualist National Union based in the U.K.

www.journeywithin.org

The Institute for Afterlife Research (IAR)

IAR was founded by Mike Pettigrew and his wife Helen Pfeiffer with the intention of breaking down the wall of fear that surrounds the issues of Death and the Afterlife.

www.mikepettigrew.com/afterlife/html/about_us.html

After Death Communication Research Foundation

Provides extensive information and resources regarding after-death communication (ADC), bereavement, grief, and life after death.

www.adcrf.org/

The International Association for Near-Death Studies (IANDS)

IANDS is the first organization in the world devoted exclusively to the study of Near-Death Experiences (NDEs) and Near-Death-like experiences. Founded in 1978, it has become the premier NDE resource for research, education, and support. Based on scientific and scholarly research roots, IANDS is the most trusted source for researchers, professional care providers, clergy, and seekers of greater meaning.

http://iands.org/home.html

The Elisabeth Kubler-Ross Foundation

The Elisabeth Kubler-Ross Foundation is a volunteer-based organization inspired by the life of psychiatrist, humanitarian, and hospice pioneer Dr. Elisabeth Kubler-Ross. Though Elisabeth is often described as the "death and dying lady" or the "creator of the Five Stages," she often referred to herself as the "life and living lady". It is in the spirit of embracing all of life, which includes death, that we further the mission and vision of Elisabeth through the work of the foundation that bears her name.

www.ekrfoundation.org/welcome/about-the-foundation/

About the Author

Tim Braun is an internationally renowned medium and has conducted over 14,000 sittings over the past twenty years. Born in Whittier, California, he is the youngest of six children. He currently lives in Orange County, and is a graduate of the University of Southern California, where he earned a BA in Interdisciplinary Studies. He has been lecturing and reading for private clients for more than twenty years. Tim has been embraced by Hollywood celebrities, renowned athletes, and international corporate leaders.

He sold out three mediumship demonstration evenings, a 700-seat venue at Pala Casino Resort, and has appeared on television in Bravo's *The Orange County Housewives* and the TLC network television show *Sin City Rules*. He has been interviewed on CBS Radio's *Sundays with Rolonda,*" *The Good Life Canada* with Jesse Dylan, *The Marilu Henner Radio Show*, *The MTV Movie Awards*, and featured in *LA.COM* and *Awareness* magazine.

Tim Braun
Live Demo Events, Private Sittings, Workshops & Training

Tim Braun offers workshops, live demo events, private sittings, and medium training classes year round. For more information, or to sign up for his free monthly newsletter, log onto:

www.TimBraun.net

TIM BRAUN
P.O. Box 984
Dana Point, California 92629 USA

You can also find Tim on:

Facebook

Tim Braun Spiritual Medium / Public Figure Twitter

YouTube

F I N D H O R N   P R E S S

Life-Changing Books

Consult our catalogue online
(with secure order facility) on
www.findhornpress.com

For information on the Findhorn Foundation:
www.findhorn.org

green press
INITIATIVE

Findhorn Press is committed to preserving ancient forests and natural resources. We elected to print this title on 30% post consumer recycled paper, processed chlorine free. As a result, for this printing, we have saved:

6 Trees (40' tall and 6-8" diameter)
3 Million BTUs of Total Energy
549 Pounds of Greenhouse Gases
2,973 Gallons of Wastewater
199 Pounds of Solid Waste

Findhorn Press made this paper choice because our printer, Thomson-Shore, Inc., is a member of Green Press Initiative, a nonprofit program dedicated to supporting authors, publishers, and suppliers in their efforts to reduce their use of fiber obtained from endangered forests.

For more information, visit www.greenpressinitiative.org

Environmental impact estimates were made using the Environmental Defense Paper Calculator. For more information visit: www.papercalculator.org.

MIX

Paper from responsible sources

FSC® C013483

www.fsc.org